THE PILGRIM WHO TRAINED HER MONKEY

WHAT THE BRAIN REVEALS ABOUT HOW TO LEAD A FULFILLED LIFE

KAROLIEN NOTEBAERT, PH.D.

The characters in this book are fictious.
Although this book is based on real conversations, the content and timing of the conversations have been adapted to fit the story line and educational purposes of the book.

Created with Vellum

To Josefien and Malou
- for being a light

When I read, I read.

PROLOGUE

Marie's Question

'Mama?'

'Yes, Marie?'

'How do I know who I am?'

I tied my shoelaces and looked up at Marie. I could see the wrinkles on her forehead, as if she still was not sure how this question had formed in her own mind.

Marie and I had started our first hiking day in Ireland. For months, we had been looking forward to walking a part of the Wicklow Way together. Up to the day we left, I had been working hard and I was in urgent need of this special break. My daughter, nature, silence, walking and talking, and the green Wicklow Mountains to guide us.

'I mean, how do I know who I am as a human being? And who do I want to become?' she asked.

I was not sure where these questions came from. Moreover, I was not sure how I could answer these questions in a few words.

'Well, first of all, you already are someone. I believe we are complete at every stage in our life, but we constantly develop and change.'

I was thinking out loud.

'How do I know then into which person I want to change?' Marie asked.

It seemed that I had caused more confusion than clarity in my daughter's mind.

'How do you know who *you* are?' she added.

I took a moment to reflect.

'Sometimes I found out who I was by knowing who I did *not* want to be.'

'What do you mean?'

'Let me give you an example. You were still a small child at the time, but for more than ten years, I had worked as a neuroscientist. This means that I collected brain data to answer research questions. One day, during my final year as a researcher, I went for lunch with a colleague. We were discussing our studies and suddenly she said, "If I only could have a few free days to spend alone with my data and analyses, I would be the happiest person on earth!" At first, I thought she was joking. But from the look on her face, I could see that this was exactly what would make her happy. Being alone with her data! The first thought that consciously crossed my mind was, "Is she in her right mind? If I had a few days' free time, I'd take a break from my data!" However, what then quickly became clear to me was that my colleague was absolutely fine and I was not. My colleague was, at least in her job, in the right place, whereas I found myself unfulfilled in my work situation. Worse, up to that moment, I thought it was usual not to be thrilled about your job. It was *work* after all. Although I am passionate about new scientific insights and listening to great scientists, something was missing in my work as a theoretical scientist. It was during that lunch break that I realised I did not want to be *this* scientist.'

There was silence.

'Does that mean you wasted ten years?' Marie asked eventually.

I laughed. 'No, most certainly not. Neuroscience still is my passion. But in order to live this passion, I don't necessarily have to work in research.'

'How did you actually know you wanted to study neuroscience?'

'Well, for that story we have to go back in time by at least 20 years. I was very curious as a child and have continued to be so. Learning and understanding the world makes me feel good. It fulfils me. When I was in my fourth year of secondary school, I could not bear the idea of spending another two years in school before going to university. I had this little book at home with all the possible courses one could sign up for at university. In the evening, I read the book over and over, checking all the courses I would like to take.'

'What type of courses?' Marie asked.

'I don't remember exactly, but I had a great interest in medicine, law and art history. Then one day, a friend of mine suggested I combine the exams of my two final years into one year so I could start university much sooner. Even though he was half-joking when he said this, I took his suggestion seriously. In the end, it's exactly what I did.'

'That sounds crazy. Wasn't that a lot of work?'

'It sounds like more work than it actually was. It was my wish to go to university that motivated me to study hard. I was not any smarter than other children of my age. It was my strong motivation that made it possible. If you really want something, you feel energised. It gave me wings. So, at sixteen, I finished my final exams and was ready to go to university.'

Marie looked at me thoughtfully.

'That is very young! Did you not miss home when you left?'

'I certainly did. Being ready intellectually does not necessarily mean that you are emotionally ready to make a certain change. Emotional developments take time – I have learned that more than once – and we cannot speed that up by studying or sharpening our understanding. I believe that your granny knew that well and tried to tell me so several times.'

I took a brief moment to reflect and mentally go back in time.

'Your granny did not say much. I remember her as a rather quiet person, staying mostly in the background rather than guiding or advising her children in a direct way. However, on the day I left home, she decided to give me a piece of good advice for life. She said: "Juliet, I know that you have a lot of potential. Just remember that the best you can accomplish in life is to use your full potential so that you become the best version of yourself".'

'To become the best version of yourself. That is not the advice I was expecting,' Marie smiled.

I laughed. 'I know. I didn't give it much consideration at the time. Don't forget that I was a teenager and had in general not too much interest in what my parents had to say. But it was exactly this advice of my mum's that significantly influenced the course of my life later on. Moreover, coming back to your question: it greatly helped me in finding out who I am.'

'It was during my very first class in neuroscience at university that I discovered a great passion for that subject. The professor explained the working of a brain cell, a neuron. I remember being captivated by the beauty with which nature has designed a neuron. It was an understanding that somehow emotionally fulfilled me. That was the moment I decided to specialise in neuroscience. One day, ten years after leaving home, I was working as a researcher and had to think back to the advice my mum had given me.'

'Becoming the best version of yourself?'

'Indeed. It was then that I asked myself the question: what does it mean "to use your full potential and to become the best version of yourself"? How can the brain develop its full potential so that you can bring your own best performance?'

'What did you find out?' Marie asked eagerly.

'Exploring this question scientifically was the start of a fascinating journey. A journey on which I learned a lot theoretically but also personally about what it means to unlock your true individual potential so you can become the truest expression of who you are. I learned about how we can approach the idea of becoming the best version of ourselves.'

Marie paused for a moment to take it all in.

'I don't think that you always are the best version of yourself,' she said with an expression of some disbelief on her face.

I poked Marie in her side and laughed out loud. 'No. I am most certainly not always the best version of myself! I believe it is a never-ending journey. However, the journey provided me with fascinating insights about how my own brain works and who I naturally want to be. These insights greatly helped me to make life decisions: important ones and less important ones.'

I paused to view the scenery and looked at Marie. Taking in the details of her face filled me with a feeling of gratitude for being here at this exact place on earth at this very moment in this exact way.

'So those years in research were most certainly not time wasted. It was during those years as a scientist that I learned so much about how the brain works. This understanding helped me to accept myself and others, just as we are. Importantly, it helped me to find out who I am.'

'Can this understanding also help me to find out who I am and what I want in life?' Marie wondered.

'I can tell you what I learned on my journey. Perhaps this will help you find your path in life,' I said.

'The path in life that makes me happy?'

'Yes, it is the path in life which fulfils us. Or in your words: understanding who you truly are and how you want to live your life.'

Our path continued up the hill. As my heartbeat was beginning to quicken and my breath became shorter, I slowed down my pace a little bit more. After climbing the hill without speaking, we took a moment to catch our breath and take in the beautiful surroundings. Smell the fresh air. Listen to the silence.

It is here that our journey began.

OUR WICKLOW WAY

DAY 1

Drumgoft – Glendalough

We had left Drumgoft about half an hour earlier and I checked the map. Soon we would be able to see the Carrawaystick Waterfall on the other side of the Valley. When the waterfall came into our view, we took our time to enjoy the miraculous sight in complete silence. When I closed my eyes, I thought I could hear the waterfall – or maybe this was just my imagination.

'It is so quiet here,' Marie noted. 'Time seems to be standing still when you are in nature and there is nobody around.'

Up to now, we had not met one single person.

'Yes, it is very quiet here,' I said as I listened to the silence. Letting my mind wander, I remembered I used to escape the house and go out into nature to find this silence and peace. I believed that it was only in situations of silence that I could calm my mind and let go of unwanted thoughts or worries. I had not understood that calming my mind or letting go of worries is a matter of finding peace in my own mind, rather than in the outside world. Also in a silent world, you can experience trouble in your mind. And even in a chaotic world, there can be peace in your mind.

'While we were walking in silence, was your mind quiet?' I asked.

. . .

'Do you mean silence in my head?' Marie gave me a frown.

I nodded.

'It's hard to say because I wasn't really paying attention to what was going on in my mind,' Marie smiled. 'But I remember it was not silent. I'm not sure it's ever silent in my head. My mind was probably wandering.'

'Did you notice any particular thoughts popping up in your mind?'

'My mind was showing me pictures of the breakfast this morning, of all the food that was placed on our breakfast table. That really was a huge Irish breakfast,' she laughed.

I pictured the breakfast we enjoyed this morning. We were hungry, which made us order a full Irish breakfast – bacon rashers, scrambled eggs, black and white pudding, beans and toast.

'The reason why I asked you about the silence in your mind is because I want to explain to you where our wandering thoughts come from. To understand who we are, let's start by looking at our thoughts. As you have noticed, it seems as if our brain is spontaneously producing a lot of thoughts that are not related to the what we are doing right now. We have this little voice in our head that is constantly talking to us. The voice just told you that the breakfast this morning was huge. I had been thinking about the book I am reading at the moment. The voice also reminds me to regularly check the map so that we don't get lost.'

'This voice seems to be talking non-stop, a bit like a busily chatting monkey,' Marie said.

I smiled.

'That is a nice image to describe the chatter of the busy voice in your mind. A small little monkey that is constantly telling us what to think, what to feel and how to behave!'

'Where does this voice come from?'

'As you have probably noticed, our brain is never at rest. This gives us the feeling that there never really is silence in our mind. As you said, the monkey seems to be chatting non-stop. A long time ago, neuroscientists thought that our brain was only active during tasks that require mental efforts, such as mathematical problems or tasks that require the processing of information and mental manipulation of information.'

'Mathematical problems do require a lot of mental energy but what do you mean with mental manipulation of information?' Marie wanted to know.

'Let me give you an example.'

I needed to think about this for a moment.

'Ok, here we go. I have a riddle for you because I know you like them. There are two people standing at a river and both want to get across to the other side. The boat can only take one person. Still, both people got to the other side. How?'

Marie took time to think.

'Can one person sit on the lap of the other person in the boat?'

'No, then the boat will sink, Marie.'

'Are there two boats?'

'That is good thinking, but no, there only is one boat,' I said. 'Shall I give you a hint?'

'No!', Marie was quick to respond. 'I want to find the answer myself. I'll think about it later on. It's not an easy riddle you picked!'

'It is a challenging one indeed. But I wanted to give you an example of a task where we have to manipulate information in our mind. When I gave you the bits of information, you processed that information. You remembered the two people, the river and the boat. You also remembered that the boat can carry only one person. Perhaps you even had an image in your mind of the river and the boat. When trying to find the answer to the riddle, you manipulated the pieces of information. You tried out different scenarios to find the answer.'

'I see, such as considering the fact that perhaps there were two boats rather than one? Or picturing the two people with one sitting on the other's lap in the boat,' Marie carried on. 'I understand. So scientists believed for a long time that our brain was only active during such tasks?'

'Indeed. They believed that the brain was in a state of "rest" when we were not actively involved in a mentally engaging task.'

'Such as relaxing on a couch?'

'Yes, just like relaxing on the couch. Or sitting in the garden. Activities that do not necessarily require a mental effort. However, about a century ago, it was discovered that our brain is never really at rest. Even when we are not completing a task or when we do not perform a certain mental activity, our brain is active. Certain parts of the brain are even more active when we are at rest. Neuroscientists call this *spontaneous activation*. This activation is automatically or spontaneously produced by our brain.'

'Spontaneous activation,' Marie said out loud. 'Indeed, I don't have to switch on my brain for it to be active. It feels that my wandering thoughts just come and go as they please.'

Leaving the forest, we had arrived in an open space where we started to climb the side of Mullacor Hill. The woods were behind us and for the first time on this hiking trip, we were treated to a wide view over the Wicklow Mountains. We looked around. I could smell the fresh air. Being surrounded by a vastness of green hills gave me an instant feeling of contentment.

'Was it my wandering mind that reminded me that my breakfast was huge?'

'It was indeed. Let's call the wandering mind the monkey in our head. I like that comparison. Do you have the feeling that you need to ask the monkey to start chatting, Marie?'

'Not really,' she thoughtfully replied. 'When we were walking in silence, the monkey just presented me with things without my doing. But why does it want to chat all the time? Why did I think about my breakfast while we were walking? Whatever the monkey said was totally unrelated to whatever we are doing now.'

'When we are not consciously directing our attention to the present, in this case walking, our mind will wander. The monkey mind might become active and might start chatting. The first type of thoughts that our brain produces is information about ourselves. In this case, you remember that you had an Irish breakfast this morning.'

'You mean a *huge* Irish breakfast?' Marie laughed.

I smiled. 'The fact that you call it *huge* is yet another type of thoughts that the monkey mind produces. You do not only remember that you had a breakfast, but you also gave this information a personal meaning. You interpreted this breakfast as *huge*. Other people might have considered this breakfast as rather small or just enough.'

'I can certainly think of a few people who would think that,' Marie cheerfully added.

'That is because they have a different brain compared to yours,' I continued. 'Your monkey calls the breakfast huge. The monkey of someone else calls the breakfast normal or even small. The monkey mind contains information about ourselves and our personal interpretation of this information. If someone tells a joke, I might understand this in a different way compared to you.'

'I might find the joke funny whereas you might find that same joke silly?' she wondered.

'Exactly. I might even find the joke insulting. The exact same wording of the joke will be interpreted in different ways depending on your unique network of thoughts,' I continued. 'Your monkey mind contains information about yourself, about what you experience and how you interpret these experiences. It is your interpretation that makes the experience truly yours. It is your unique, personal experience.'

We took a moment to stand still and drink some water.

'It is exactly this personal interpretation that results in a feeling. Your monkey mind interprets the joke as funny, whereas mine does not. As a result of this interpretation, you will laugh and feel jolly whereas I feel confused or even insulted. The exact same information, namely the joke, was told to both of us but we both interpret this information in a unique way. As a result, we experience a different emotion.'

'Look there,' Marie called out. 'Do you see those sheep?'

I smiled. Seeing those sheep made my monkey instantly rattle on. I remembered one of my first trips to Ireland. I had rented a car and had driven to the West of Ireland to discover Achill Island and to walk along the Atlantic Ocean. The Atlantic Ocean at that part of the world feels rough and particularly deserted. It was challenging to drive on the left hand side of the road. Adding to this challenge, I noticed that roads can occasionally be used by sheep. Sheep seem to be everywhere in Ireland. I looked at Marie, who seemed lost in thought.

'Do you remember when you ran the 800 meter race a few months ago, Marie? How did you feel?' I asked turning away from my thoughts about sheep.

'Well, I felt very proud when I won the race. But I remember I felt very nervous at the start.'

'Why did you feel nervous?'

'I felt nervous because it was an important race and I knew that many people were watching. But I also knew that I trained hard and that I was well prepared, which helped me to be less nervous and to concentrate.'

'I remember you felt nervous. I also remember how you, right before the race, took a deep breath and focused. Imagine now that your trainer would have told you that you had no chance of winning that race. Would this have changed the race?' I challenged Marie.

'I don't think I would have done so well,' she quickly responded. 'I would have lost confidence in myself.'

'Does this mean that you would have lost your actual athletic talent and the effect of the hard training would have been lost?' I rhetorically asked.

She paused.

. . .

'No. Of course not. It would not have affected my actual talent,' she asserted.

'You are right. Your talent is your talent. Nobody can take this away from you. But believing in your talent is half the success. Your thoughts about your talent however can interfere with your performance. Thoughts can play a significant role in blocking us in our unique potential. On the other hand, thoughts can play a significant role in unlocking our potential so we can become the best version of who we uniquely are. We can talk more about this later on. For now, I want to explain to you that it is our own thoughts and our beliefs that can decide which feelings we experience. If you think you are not good at mathematics, it can affect your motivation and you might not do well in a test. The negative feeling that will be caused by your own thoughts will cause a large energy loss in your brain. This energy loss will negatively influence your actual performance,' I explained. 'Some people have grown up with the belief that they are not good at, for example, science. Perhaps they have been told at home that science is "only for the very smart students", or perhaps girls heard that "science is a boything".'

'But there is something to this - if we talk about great scientific discoveries, it was often a man who played the most important role in the discovery, right?' Marie pointed out.

'Can you name a few, Marie?'

She took a moment to think.

'Well, we have Einstein, Darwin, Newton, ... Oh and Tesla!' she recounted.

'Indeed, but there were also fantastic female scientists. Have you heard about Marie Curie?' I asked.

'I have. Wasn't she a Nobel Prize winner?'

'Yes she was. She won a Nobel Prize for Chemistry in the early 1900s for her breakthrough research on radioactivity. She won many more prestigious prizes for her pioneering research. Also Dorothy Hodgkin was an extraordinary researcher. She, too, won the Nobel Prize for Chemistry for her ground breaking work.'

'Still, it seems that there are more famous male scientists than female scientists,' Marie argued.

'That is the case. If you search for the most famous scientists of the past, you will see that there are more famous male than female scientists. Especially in the past, education was something meant for boys. Girls were expected to stay at home, take care of the family and household. The little money for education that many families had was invested in their sons.'

'I believe that is very unfair,' Marie exclaimed.

'You consider this as unfair. In the past, this was what many people thought was the right thing to do. As a result, more male scientists were supported in their academic development. Consequently, we have heard more about male than female scientists. These experiences have shaped our beliefs throughout our life. As a result, in our brain, the connection between "male" and "science" is much stronger compared to the connection between "female" and "sci ence",' I explained.

'And because your beliefs are shaped in this way, your monkey might tell you that science is more a boy than a girl thing,' Marie added.

'Exactly. This can consciously but often also unconsciously drive us. The truth is that the qualities that are needed to perform in the field of science are equally well distributed in girls and boys. It is our thoughts, however, that shape our future. Even without being aware of our thoughts, our beliefs will influence our choices and consequently our life's path. If we believe that boys are better at science than girls, we might decide not to pursue scientific topics. This often unconscious choice sadly results in lost potential. I am very certain that if, throughout the development of humankind, women had had the same educational chances, we would have seen as many female as male scientists. It is our own beliefs and thoughts that play a significant role in shaping our future. Luckily, we have the capacity to become much more aware of our thoughts and create a space to master our thoughts.'

~

I COULD SEE Marie was lost in her own thoughts.

'Why don't we take a small break here? Let's drink something and check the map,' I suggested.

After drinking some water, we decided to sit down and relax. Marie found herself a big stone to sit on. She closed her eyes. The sun was shining on her face.

'You know,' she said after a few minutes, 'my monkey is chatting constantly. I have not really noticed this before, but even now, when I am closing my eyes, he is chatting. It seems that I can't really shut him up.'

I smiled. 'I know, Marie,' I replied. 'It is our active and busy network of thoughts. We are capable of shutting up the monkey and getting it to tell us something we would like to hear. But that I will explain to you later. For now, remember that our thoughts are very powerful. In fact, even our very own destiny starts with a single thought.'

Watch your thoughts
They become your words
Watch your words
They become your actions
Watch your actions
They become your habits
Watch your habits
They become your character
Watch your character
It becomes your destiny

(Mahatma Ghandi)

'What else does the monkey mind do?' Marie wondered.

After we had taken a moment to catch our breath, we had continued our walk.

'Our brain also produces our ideas and opinions about others. Let me give you an example. Do you know what I was thinking or feeling when you ran the 800 meter race?' I asked her.

'I know you felt very proud when I won the race. Before the race, I think you thought that I could win it.'

'How do you know that?'

Marie reflected. 'I'm not sure, I just took a good guess. You are my mother after all.'

'This is exactly the second type of thoughts that the brain produces. It contains information about what we believe others are thinking and feeling. When I am holding a seminar and I see people frowning, my monkey might interpret this as confusion or disinterest in those people.

Alternatively, my monkey might read their faces as a deep reflection on the topic that I am talking about. If my monkey tells me those people are not interested, this might lead to an insecure feeling within myself. On the other hand, if my monkey tells me those people are deeply reflecting on the content of my seminar, I might feel good and motivated. As you see, the thoughts that we have about others and the ideas we have about how they feel can impact our own feelings. These feelings in turn can lead to actions. If I feel insecure, I might decide to change the topic of the seminar or take a break. If I feel good and motivated, on the other hand, I might lead my listeners in another exercise. What these people *really* are thinking and feeling is not crucial for my own feelings and actions. What determines my next move, is what my monkey tells me they are thinking and how they are feeling.'

'The monkey plays a very important role. His opinions about myself and others shape how I feel and behave. Can I not decide what the monkey tells me?'

'We are all born with a certain personality that greatly contributes to what we experience. Let me give you an example. Some people are born with a strong need for social connection. These are people who feel deeply fulfilled when they can spend time with others. It makes them feel good. This rewarding feeling teaches them to more often seek social interaction and connection with others. What we experience as positive, we will try to experience again,' I said.

'But don't we all want to be connected with others?' Marie seemed a little confused.

'I do believe so. We all have a need to be loved and spend time with others. It is a basic human need. However, the strength of this basic human need is different in all of us.

Some people have a strong need for love and social connection, others have a much less strong need for love and connection. It is the strength of this need that will shape our thoughts and consequently our experiences. If we are born with a strong desire to spend a lot of time with others, this will make us look for situations where we can spend time with others. The monkey will tell us that spending time with others gives us a good feeling. We are not always aware of the monkey, but it is there. As a consequence, we will select certain situations. These situations result in certain experiences, which become part of the networks in our brain. The more a situation is repeated, the more it becomes part of your monkey mind. These situations become very strong connections in your brain. They gain power in leading your actions.'

~

MARIE STOPPED WALKING and took out an apple from the backpack.

'I am not sure if I understand this correctly. Does the brain constantly change?' Marie thought out loud.

'Indeed it does. This is what they call neuroplasticity. It was strongly believed for a long time that the brain was not capable of changing once you were an adult. However, many recent studies have shown that the brain is able to change throughout your entire life. In fact, you can change the brain even when you are one hundred years old. I heard this story once about an old man who learned how to speak Chinese at the age of 90!'

'Was he Chinese?' Marie chuckled.

I laughed. 'I don't remember where he was from, but he was not Chinese. He fell in love with a Chinese lady. I suppose his motivation to learn the language was very strong,' I continued.

'Let's have a look at how the brain is structured. The building blocks of our brain are brain cells or neurons. These neurons have a long tail with which they connect to other neurons. Each neuron can make connections with up to 10 000 other neurons. Given that your brain consists of up to 100 billion neurons, you can imagine how many connections in the brain are possible. Thus, the brain is a very complex, dense network of connections between brain cells. What I want to say here is that we can influence these connections. This is neuroplasticity. One possible way for us to change connections is to strengthen or weaken connections. Imagine you are learning Chinese. At the start, the Chinese signs do not mean anything to you. This means that, in your complex connection of brain cells, a certain Chinese sign is not connected to any other word or picture in your brain. During the learning process, you learn that a certain Chinese sign means "exit". In fact, if you look closely at the sign, it does look like an exit. With a lot of effort, you try to mentally connect this sign with the meaning of "exit" in your mind. Through this mental process, a weak connection between the Chinese sign and "exit" is formed. After repeated practice, this connection will become much stronger until a certain point where you recognize the Chinese sign for "exit" immediately without any mental effort.'

'So this is how I learned my math tables as a young child!' Marie stated.

'That is correct. This is a very simple example to understand how brain plasticity works. When emotions are involved in this process, the learning curve can look very different!'

'Do you mean that it was easier for the old man to learn Chinese because he was in love?'

'Being in love can be a great motivation for learning something. The man loved the lady very much and desperately wanted to communicate with her. This strong motivation significantly helped him to study a completely new language at the age of 90. But also in different ways, emotions can speed up a learning process,' I said.

'I see. When I understand why I have to learn something, I find it easier to motivate myself to learn compared to simply rehearsing some facts without understanding why I have to do this,' Marie added.

'Understanding why something is important to us does indeed help our motivation to learn. You know, sometimes it only takes one experience to learn something for the rest of your life,' I continued. 'How do you know not to drink hot soup?' I asked Marie.

'Well, I remember burning my tongue drinking hot soup as a child.' Marie gave me a painful expression.

'Exactly. This burning caused a strong feeling of pain. In your brain, the connection between "hot soup" and "do not drink" or "be careful" became very strong after that painful experience. And believe me, Marie, I had told you many times before to be very careful with hot soup. My telling you did not have that same effect. I could have told you one million times to be careful, but it is the actual emotional experience that right away resulted in a strong connection between "hot soup" and "do not drink" or "be careful". I am your mother and I will always warn you. But I have also understood that many things are learnt most effectively and efficiently when you experience them for yourself.'

'Does that mean I do not really help Louise when I warn her that she drives too wildly on her bike?' Marie worried.

I smiled.

'Well, first of all. You are her older sister. I do not think Louise likes to listen to her older sister. But to come back to what I said about learning: If a connection in our brain is strong enough, it will guide us. For this connection to be strong enough for us to actually change something, emotions do help a great deal. If Louise would experience that another person was hurt due to wild cycling, this might give her some concern. This feeling then might strengthen the connection between "wild driving" and "dangerous" in her own brain, possible resulting in a calmer, safer cycling style.'

I paused for a moment.

'It is the same with adults,' I continued. 'Sometimes it is obvious to others in our environment that we are in an unhealthy situation but somehow it does not motivate us to change. Even when *we know* that we are in an unhealthy situation.'

'Such as smoking,' Marie stated. 'We all know that smoking is unhealthy, also the smokers, but still they keep on smoking.'

'Yes, such as smoking. This *knowing* is often not powerful enough to stop the addiction. Think about my colleague Stephan. He used to smoke a lot. One day a few years ago, the doctor diagnosed that Stephan potentially had a severe problem with his heart that urgently needed further medical investigation. Whether or not this medical condition was actually caused by smoking, I am not sure. Stephan, however, mentally made the connection between the potential heart problem and the smoking. He quit smoking the next day. All of a sudden, the personal emotion that was involved in this experience resulted in a very strong connection between "smoking" and "dangerous for me" in his brain. This connection was strong enough to help him quit smoking. *Feeling* you are in an unhealthy situation is much more powerful than simply *knowing or understanding* it,' I concluded.

We had decided to sit in the sun for some time and enjoy the surroundings. I checked the map and drank some water. I took an apple and ate it in silence. Marie put on a light scarf. The sun was out but the wind was fresh.

'So it will not help our neighbour if I repeatedly tell her that smoking is unhealthy?' Marie asked.

'I'm afraid not. Smoking is just one example but there are many more,' I replied.

'Unfortunately, through my work I have come in contact with a lot of people who are overworked. They work very long hours in a job they do not like. Due to the long hours, they seldom see their family and have no time to do the things they really enjoy. They miss out on the things that make them happy.'

'Why would they lead a life that makes them unhappy?' Marie asked while picking up a stone she found in the grass.

'Through conversations with them, it became clear to me that those people do not necessarily realize that they are in a mentally unhealthy situation. They complain. If you ask them why they keep on living this way, you often hear them say they need the money for their car, to pay off their house, to pay for their children's education, to save for their pension, and so on.'

'But these things do cost a lot of money, right?'

'Indeed, but I wonder whether we can even enjoy the house, the car, the retirement or the education when we are unhappy in the process of getting there. How can I expect you to live a happy life with an expensive education with which you might end up working too long hours in a job you do not like? This does not mean that I do not want you to enjoy a good education. If studying makes you happy, you should study. If it makes you happy to work as a teacher, as a banker or in a bakery, I believe that this is what you should do. Ideally, your choices reflect your own true wishes and not the wishes or expectations of others or society. Some people have worked their full adult life in jobs they don't like to fulfil the expectations of others. They studied something because their parents expected them to.'

'Or because they did not know yet what made them happy.'

Marie threw her stone away.

'Indeed, when you are young and have not yet collected many life experiences, it might not be easy to have an insight in what makes you happy. So, let's assume that as a young person you choose studies based on expectations of others or simply because you did not know any better. These studies lead to a job. At the start, you enjoy the job because it allows you to learn new skills, you become part of a social network and the financial means allow you to live independently. After a few years of work, you notice that you do not enjoy that particular job as much as you did at the start. You have learned the most important skills, the social network now includes colleagues you do not like and you have become used to the money you earn. The job that was once new and exciting has become more or less routine. After some more years of this, you occasionally allow yourself to reflect on why you do what you do. You might admit to yourself that you are not happy in the job but quickly the monkey reminds you of the mortgage you are paying, the lifestyle you have developed and so on. After so many years of work, these habits have become very strong connections in your brain. As I mentioned to you before, the more you repeat a certain pattern of behaviour, thoughts or emotions, the more powerful the connections become. These powerful connections drive you every day. It is very difficult to break those habits and start something new.'

'Will a strong emotion help you to change? Such as the old man who learned Chinese?'

'I suppose so. Certain experiences can lead to such a strong emotion that it enables you to change an engrained habit from one day to another. Again, it is the strong *feeling* that enables you to change, not the understanding. Being intellectually ready for a change does not necessarily mean that you are emotionally ready for a change. This emotional readiness is of crucial important to make a change happen. At the end of the day, it is mainly your emotions that drive you and give you the motivation and energy to carry out change,' I replied.

'Can you give me an example?'

I took a moment to reflect.

'ALTHOUGH THERE ARE LUCKILY many people who enjoy their job and receive great fulfilment in working hard, I have met people where this was not the case. Vanessa is one person who pops into my mind here. Vanessa changed her life on the day her brother died. I had met Vanessa about three years ago when I got to know her as a very hardworking lady. She had a fantastic career. Nevertheless, she did not enjoy her work and mostly felt unfulfilled. When I asked her what did make her happy, she said that she has a great passion for travelling. She always wanted to travel but kept on making excuses for why it was not the right time. When she started to work, she wanted to give herself a good start in her career by working long hours and taking on ambitious projects. After a few years, she had saved enough money to undertake a trip around the world, but then she said she did not want to miss her next promotion by taking time off. A few years after that, she had taken on so much responsibility in her job that leaving her job for a few months was not an option anymore. She came home late most nights, too exhausted to engage in the activities that she really enjoyed. To compensate for the stress she experienced, she started to use her money to buy things that gave her an instant good feeling. She bought an expensive car, designer handbags and shoes to make her feel better.'

'How does an expensive handbag make you feel better?'

'In Vanessa's case, it was the impulsive buying that gave her a short burst of feeling good. It is a powerful and persistent urge that we feel to buy something immediately, in an impulse. Most of us experience that at times, I suppose. Do you remember we were in that sports store last month and you really wanted to buy those new runners?'

'I do indeed. They were looking great. Luckily, we did not buy them because I have two pairs at home,' Marie chuckled.

'But still, you felt the urge to buy the runners, right? Engaging in impulsive buying can give people an immediate feeling of arousal, more specifically a rewarding sensation. When you saw the runners, the reward system in your brain became active and produced dopamine. Dopamine is a neurotransmitter. You remember I told you that the brain consists of many brain cells or neurons that connect with each other, right? These neurons can communicate with each other. They pass on messages by releasing chemicals, which are called neurotransmitters. When neurotransmitters are released, a message will be passed on to a connected neuron.'

'So what do they say to each other, these neurons?' Marie winked at me.

'The release of the neurotransmitter could for example activate the next neuron. This neuron might pass on the message to his connections. In a fraction of a second, a full activation pattern will emerge in your brain. This activation pattern has a particular meaning to us. Why don't we try this out?'

~

MARIE STOPPED WALKING.

'O.K., how do we do this?'

'Just close your eyes for a moment and try to visualize Louise. Can you do that?'

'Yes, I see her face in my mind.'

'What is she doing?'

'She is giving me a funny face.'

Marie smiled.

'Now open your eyes again,' I said. 'The images and thoughts that you have in your mind are all unique activation patterns in your brain. The picture of your sister is a particular pattern of activation. Louise giving you a funny face is another, yet similar pattern of activation in your brain. If I could link these unique activation patterns in your brain to what they mean to you, I would be reading your mind, right?'

'That is scary! And I certainly would not want that,' she called out.

'Going back to the impulsive buying. When you saw those runners, the reward system in your brain became active. The monkey became excited and told you that, at that very moment, you *really* wanted those runners. If you would have bought those runners, it would have activated the reward system even more and you would have felt a short burst of feeling good. Typically, this good feeling does not last long, especially for things we do not need at all. By the time we come home, the good feeling might have evaporated.'

'And we wasted the money!'

'Yes, we would have wasted the money. Even worse, once we find out that we really did not need that product and how much money we spent on buying it, we can even start feeling guilty,' I continued.

'So Vanessa wasted a lot of money on her handbags and shoes?'

'Well, some people are really interested in design and can spend days looking for the right handbag or shoes. It is their real interest and they spend a lot of time using and enjoying these purchases. For Vanessa, however, this was not the case. She engaged in impulsive buying to compensate for the work stress she experienced. She felt mentally exhausted and not fulfilled through the job she did. To cope with this feeling of emptiness, she impulsively purchased handbags and shoes that gave her a short burst of feeling good.'

'The activation of the reward system,' Marie concluded.

'You are right. Although she felt a rush of reward when she bought a particular handbag, the feeling of emptiness recurred in very short order.'

Marie seemed to be lost in her thoughts for a moment.

'That is very sad, isn't it?' she suddenly said. 'I hope I will not waste that much time in my life.'

'It is easier said than done. For outsiders, such as Vanessa's parents or friends, it might have been obvious that Vanessa was not happy in her life. And in fact, to some degree, Vanessa was aware of that! Whenever she came to these insights, she made up excuses, such as not wanting to miss the next level in her career or having to pay for a mortgage. "I simply can't make the change! I have already invested so much time and energy into this!", she would tell herself. Changing our belief system to match our behaviour is easier than changing the behaviour.'

'You say that Vanessa was justifying the behaviour that did not make her happy?'

'She did to a certain extent,' I replied. 'I will explain more. The cognitive dissonance theory explains this process well. This psychological theory was put forward by a researcher called Leon Festinger. In short, we want our thoughts and beliefs to be consonant with our behaviour. If we, for example, strongly believe in a healthy lifestyle, ideally, we also actively live a healthy lifestyle. This means that we might eat healthy food and regularly exercise. Simply put, what we do matches our beliefs. If, however, we end up eating a bag of crisps during a movie, there will be a discrepancy between our behaviour and our belief system. You believe in a healthy life style, still you are eating a full bag of crisps. This discrepancy as you can probably see creates an internal conflict. A conflict in your mind. There are several ways to resolve this conflict.'

'Do you mean not eating the bag of crisps?' Marie suggested.

'Yes, that's a good example. This would mean that you

solve the internal conflict by changing your behaviour. However, research has shown that we more often resolve the conflict by changing our thoughts or beliefs. In this example, we could lower the importance of our dissonant behaviour by saying "oh, it is only a bit of crisps. That won't hurt" or we give the dissonant behaviour a new meaning that fits our belief that a healthy lifestyle is important.'

'You mean for example by stating that eating crisps is healthy?'

I smiled. 'Perhaps this is a bit of an extreme example, but yes, that is what I mean. We can also do this in a more subtle way, by saying "you know, my uncle ate a bag of crisps every evening and lived until the age of 93! Apart from the rare cold, he never was sick!". Do you know what I mean?'

Marie reflected. 'I think I do. So the excuses that Vanessa made up were meant to reduce her internal conflict?'

'I believe so. The moment that she allowed herself to become aware of her unhappiness in her job, she noticed the discrepancy between her belief that she wanted to lead a happy life while feeling unhappy with the choices she made in life, namely working long hours for a job she did not particularly enjoy.'

'And Vanessa solved this internal conflict by changing her beliefs. She started to believe that the work was important to pay for her house, her car and getting a promotion in her job?'

'Exactly. And you know what, Marie? It is so much easier to adapt your beliefs to your behaviour than to actually change your behaviour. Making a change requires a lot of courage – or a strong emotional readiness.'

'Did you not say that she did change her lifestyle in the end?' Marie asked with hope in her voice.

'She did. I told you before that it is a strong emotion that can motivate us to actually break out of an unhealthy pattern. Two years after I met Vanessa, her brother was diagnosed with cancer. Her brother was still very young, in his thirties. Only three months after the diagnosis, he passed away. The day that Vanessa's brother died, she experienced a mixture of strong emotions. She felt devastated for losing her brother. At the same time, she felt regret for not having spent more time with him to tell him how much he meant to her. Another powerful emotion she felt was the desire not to die unhappy. Looking at her own life, she suddenly realized more than ever how much time she had wasted on working in a job that made her unhappy, in order to buy things she did not need or really enjoy. In fact, I should say: she suddenly *felt* how much time she had wasted. It was this strong feeling that motivated her to change. She realized that the wealthy lifestyle she could afford was not necessarily fulfilling her.'

'So how did she make the change?'

'After her brother passed away, Vanessa used some of her savings to travel around the world. She sold her car and sublet her luxurious apartment. Once you make such an emotionally powerful decision, life will always show you a way. You will not feel the need to constantly re-think your decision. It will be made and your path will become visible as long as you allow yourself to see it. It is your emotional readiness that will naturally lead to a change, which I personally do not see as a choice but more as an organic development of ourselves.'

'I do not want to wait for something terrible to happen before I change an unhealthy habit.'

'I know. Let's talk later on about how to avoid wasting precious time. But first of all, I am ready for lunch. How about you?'

'I am hungry!' Marie replied. We found a big stone to sit on and took off our backpack. I felt the pressure on my back drop away. Although we had packed lightly, we still carried our own luggage along our Hiking tour. I had taken most of the weight and was happy to give my shoulders a break. I closed my eyes, massaged my shoulders and felt the tension leave. My body relaxed.

'Where is Vanessa now?'

I briefly reflected.

'I am not sure where in the world she is, but she certainly is in a nice place, Marie. A happy place.'

Marie smiled.

'You still have not told me how we can unlock our unique potential,' Marie reminded me.

We had finished our lunch break and were back on the road. At this moment, we were walking along the vast grasslands of the Wicklow Mountains. As the grassland can get very swampy when it rains, this part of the Wicklow Way is built of wooden beams, called a board walk. The wooden beams are all covered in very thin iron wire to prevent slipping when it rains or when it is moist outside. Looking down at the small metal hooks that are used to attach the iron wire to the wood, I tried to imagine the workers and the effort it took to hammer thousands of metal hooks into the board walk. It must have been an amazing job, I thought.

'Are you listening, mama?'

Marie interrupted my thoughts.

'Which way do we go?'

The board walk formed a T-junction and I studied the map.

'The Wicklow Way goes right,' Marie pointed at the Wicklow Way sign.

'Either we follow the Wicklow Way or we walk a longer tour via The Spink, which offers spectacular views,' I said while looking at the description of the trail.

'Let's walk up The Spink, I am not tired yet,' Marie suggested. 'So, you still have not told me what it means to unlock your unique potential.'

'Right. Let's see, what have you learned up to now?'

Marie collected her thoughts. 'Well, you told me that the brain is never at rest. We have this spontaneous activation in our brain. I have learned that the constant voice in my brain is my monkey mind. It chats a lot and tells us what to think, feel and how to behave.'

'Very well said. Do you still remember what kind of thoughts the monkey mind produces?'

'The monkey mind contains information about ourselves but also about others,' she added.

'Exactly, our brain contains information about the events we have experienced, how we think about ourselves and how we feel. Also, as you said, we have ideas of what other people are feeling and thinking.'

'Oh, and I will never forget Vanessa and that I do not want to wait for something terrible to happen before I change an unhealthy habit!' Marie called out.

Marie's enthusiasm made me smile.

'Before I tell you more about unlocking your true individual potential, I will finish my explanation about the monkey mind. The third type of thoughts that our monkey mind produces are thoughts about the past and about the future. We remember details about events that we have experienced but we can also imagine or speculate about what the future will bring. If it comes to the life that you have lived up to now, what are the events that come to your mind quickest?' I asked her.

While Marie reflected on my question, I took a moment to catch my breath. We were now half-way climbing The Spinc and my body told me to reduce my walking pace. I looked around. I smelled the air. I tried to feel the silence. As far as I could see, I could only see nature. The green Wicklow Mountains. The higher we had walked, the windier it had become. I stopped walking and closed my eyes. I could hear the wind and feel the moist air on my face. The sun had gone behind some clouds and a fog had appeared.

'Are you okay?' Marie wanted to know. She had kept on walking and the distance between us had become larger. I opened my eyes and rejoined her on our path.

'Yes, I am. Have you found an answer? What are the life events you easily remember?' I asked her again.

'It is not an easy question,' she answered. 'There are so many little events that my monkey mind brought up, but if I think of the events that I remember well.... I think of our skiing trip last year. Or the last school play I performed in.'

'Why did you pick these events?'

'Well, the skiing trip really was good fun. We had a great time, remember? And the play – I think I remember it well because I was very nervous, especially because I knew my family was in the audience.'

'Emotions play an important role in remembering events that we experience. Those events that trigger an emotional state in our brain are usually remembered better than those that are not connected with an emotional state,' I explained to her.

'Do you remember where and with whom we were when we found out about the terrorist attacks at the airport in Brussels?'

'Yes, I do,' she replied quickly. 'We were visiting granny in Belgium. We were sitting in the living room when we heard the news. Granny had switched on the television to find out more. I remember you were sitting on the couch and you looked worried.'

'I felt worried, indeed. Do you also remember what we did the day before or the day after?'

I could see thinking wrinkles form on her forehead.

'No, I don't,' she eventually replied. 'Why is that?'

'Events that trigger an emotion in our brain are usually remembered better compared to events that have no emotional meaning to us. Do you remember what the brain looks like?'

'I do. It looks grey and is full of wrinkles.'

'The outer layer of the brain is grey indeed. This layer of our brain is about 2 to 4 millimetres thin and is called the cortex. It is shaped by many folds, called fissures. The cortex plays an essential role in many of our functions. Although all parts of the cortex work together, there are certain parts that can be clearly linked to specific functions. We have a part of the brain that is responsible for sight, one for hearing, one for smelling and one for feeling. For example, the outer back part of your cortex is responsible for processing visual information, for your sight. If this part of your brain is damaged, you are cortically blind. Your brain cannot process and interpret the information that reaches the brain through your eyes.'

'So even with eyes that work perfectly well, I can still be blind,' Marie stated. 'In fact, this means that I see with my brain, not with my eyes.'

'The cortex of the brain indeed plays a significant role. That is why it is called cortical blindness when we cannot see due to damage of the cortex. Seeing and recognizing something happens in our brain. We do need our eyes of course to catch the visual input. This visual input is then sent to the brain where it is processed and interpreted,' I said. 'For example, your eyes see the hiking map. This information is processed in the back of our brain, where the information is organized in colours, shades, shapes, and so on. These bits of information are further distributed and processed throughout the cortex. This particular activation pattern in our brain means "map",' I continued.

'Just like me having an activation pattern in my brain that means "Louise",' Marie remembered having pictured Louise in her mind earlier.

'Indeed, we can even mentally activate that particular pattern when Louise is not around. Or when you close your eyes, you might still have an image of the map in your mind,' I added.

Marie took some time to think.

'Why do we sometimes get confused? I mean, it has happened to me before that I think I saw a person I know but when looking closer, I noticed it was someone else,' Marie said.

'Well, just as you explained earlier, also the people we know have a particular pattern of activation in our brain. If we see a person that looks like Louise, our brain might fill in the gaps and trigger the activation pattern that is connected to Louise. Or our brain will wrongfully tell us that we see Louise. When you look again or closer, new information might reach your brain that will correct the activation pattern in your brain. This correction will be processed and your brain will now tell you this person is not Louise.'

'Does it also work like that for hearing sounds or feeling things?' Marie wondered.

'It works in a similar way. Information reaches our senses through our eyes, ears, nose, skin or tongue. This information is, apart from smells, filtered in our brain. This means that information that is regarded as irrelevant will be filtered out and information that is considered as relevant or important will be transferred to the cortex where it is further interpreted.'

'How can information be irrelevant?'

'Let me give you an example. Are you, at this very moment, aware of how your shoes are pressing against your feet?'

Marie smiled and looked at her feet. 'Well, I am now, because you ask. But before that, I was not aware of my feet.'

'Because consciously feeling your feet was not relevant to you a moment ago. When we bring our attention to feeling our feet or when our feet hurt, for example, we will notice them. But in general, this information is not particularly interesting for the situation you are in. Therefore, you will not be conscious of this information. If your brain would consciously process all information that is captured by our senses, we would be overwhelmed.'

'I see. Thus, external information reaches our senses and, depending on what the brain finds relevant, information is either filtered out or processed further. What else does the cortex do?'

'Some parts of the cortex are called association areas

because they combine information coming from different senses,' I explained. 'Let's assume that I would blindfold you and have you guess the taste of a soup. You take a spoon full of soup and concentrate on your taste. You clearly taste tomato soup. Even better, you also smell tomato soup. But then you take off your blindfold, open your eyes and you see that the soup is green. What answer will you give me?'

'Euhm. That is strange. Tomato soup is red so I would be totally confused,' she replied quickly.

'Indeed, our experience has learned that tomato soup is red and also has a particular taste and smell. In the association areas of the brain, information from our senses is combined so that it can produce a perceptual experience, such as eating tomato soup. These association areas are connections between brain structures that process different pieces of information. These connections form a network so that colour, taste, smell, sound and sense can be combined into a full experience. In our brain, we have a clear representation of eating tomato soup which contains information about how tomato soup looks, how it tastes and how it smells. If one of these pieces of information does not fit, such as the colour of the soup, it is a very odd experience, right?' I continued. 'By smelling croissants in the bakery, we can easily guess it is a croissant we smell, we know what it tastes like and we know a fresh croissant crunches a little when you take a bite.'

'It makes me feel hungry!' Marie laughed.

We had now reached the top of The Spinc. The extra effort was worth the spectacular view we had. We had a 360° view of the Wicklow Mountains National Park. This view made me feel small but whole at the same time. It is my feeling of completeness, of being part of a whole. The feeling of being at the right place on earth, of being at the right place in my mind, the feeling of all is right and fits perfectly. It is my feeling of pure trust.

I closed my eyes and smelled the air. I knew that, soon, we would have a breathtaking view over Glendalough Valley.

'So the cortex of our brain processes information coming from our senses and also combines it,' Marie summarizes. 'How about tasks, such as mathematics or learning a new language?'

'These are two examples of what we call higher cognitive functions. Also these are functions of the cortex. Planning, organizing, analysing information, thinking about solutions, learning something new, ... These are all higher functions for which we need a well-functioning cortex,' I stated. 'Not to forget that the cortex allows us to move around and walk.'

'It is strange to think that an organ so small is important for so many essential functions. That is very fascinating,' Marie remarked.

At this very moment we were treated to our first view of Glendalough Valley. We took a break to take in the beautiful view. We could see the Upper Lake and further down the Lower Lake of Glendalough. Without any doubt, this is my favourite view of the Wicklow Way. Also here, a board walk is constructed all the way down into the Valley. Not only does the board walk offer a stable path to walk on, it also triggers a playful feeling in me. As a child, I could not resist walking on low walls along the sidewalk rather than on the sidewalk itself. As an adult, I have grown out of the urge to turn the sidewalks into my playground. But here, this simple boardwalk re-activates these memories and associated cheerful feeling. Marie was happily hopping in front of me, stretching out her arms sideways and started to sing a song. Looking back at me regularly, I noticed the serenity on her face. I promised myself to always remember this moment. I observed her and wished for the moment not to pass.

A LITTLE BIT FURTHER, we passed by a lady with a green hat, who we had met several times before today. Both Marie and I joyfully greeted her, which was reciprocated with a big smile.

Marie and I started to descend into Glendalough Valley. The path down was constructed of the same wooden beams, in many cases built into steps going down. Passing by many people walking up the stairs, Marie mentioned how lucky we were to not have to walk up all those stairs coming from the Valley down below. Feeling the tiredness in my own legs, I reminded her how much we had been climbing today. We were close to the bottom of the thousands of stairs when we cheerfully greeted a couple walking up the stairs. Both were breathing heavily and I could see the exhaustion on their face. 'You are nearly at the top!' I said. 'Really?' the lady hopefully asked. 'Not exactly,' I said, 'but you are doing very well!'. The lady and young man laughed.

'That was a little mean,' Marie argued.

'Well, perhaps it was a little mean. But both laughed and the positive emotion has given them a short boost of energy. Also, they will still remember having met us when they reach the top!'

'Because you made them laugh, I see,' Marie said.

After a long descent, we reached a wide riverside path guiding us along the Poulanass river and waterfall. We decided to take a break at the riverside. The sound of the river and waterfall stopped our talking. I found a rock to sit on and closed my eyes. I noticed that by closing my eyes and bringing my full awareness to the sound of the water, the quality of the sound changed. Marie started to play with a few stones, building a small tower until the stones fell down.

'So why do I remember events that are connected with an emotion better?'

I opened my eyes and saw the curious expression on her face.

'You remember I told you about the cortex, right? As I said, the cortex is responsible for processing sensory information that comes from our senses and combining that information into a perceptual experience. The cortex also enables us to use our body and to move, which happens in the motor cortex. Also higher cognitive functions, such as planning, organizing, analysing information and thinking of solutions are driven by the cortex.'

'These are many functions for only a thin layer of brain cells,' Marie concluded.

'Underneath the cortex, there are many more structures. These are called the subcortical structures. Sub is the Latin word for "under".'

'Because these structures are underneath the cortex,' Marie said out loud.

'Exactly. Even though these structures are underneath the cortex, they are well connected to the cortex so that all parts can influence each other and work together. Some of these subcortical structures form the limbic system together.'

'Let me guess, this system plays an important role in our emotional life?'

I smiled.

'Indeed, we have finally arrived at the part of the brain that plays an important role in our emotional life. The limbic system contains several structures, each with a particular function. Let me tell you more about the ones that are relevant for answering your question. One small part of the limbic system is the thalamus. It plays an important role in our consciousness and our sleep. The thalamus is also called the sensory relay station of our brain.'

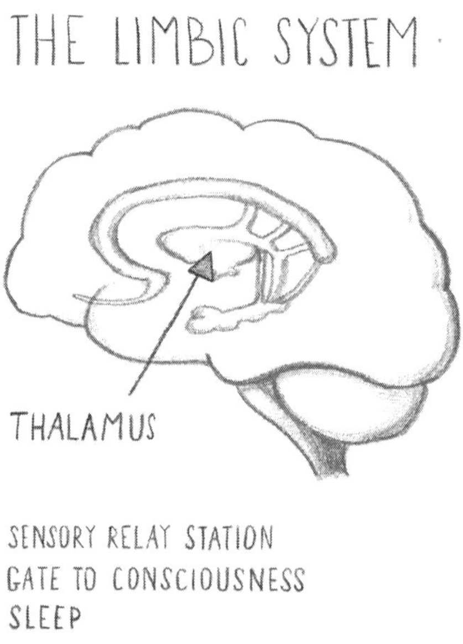

Marie frowned. 'The sensory relay station? What does that mean?'

'I told you before that through our senses, these are the eyes, ears, nose, skin and tongue we receive information from the outside world, right? This information is received by our senses and is sent to the thalamus. The thalamus will then operate as a relay station. It will first decide whether the information is relevant or not. If the information is relevant, the thalamus will send the information to other parts of the brain for further processing. If the information is regarded as irrelevant for the moment, these bits of information will be filtered out.'

'Like when you asked me today whether I was aware of the pressure of my shoes on my feet?'

'When this information is not important to us, the thalamus will filter out that information and we will not consciously process it.'

'Let's do a small experiment and play with our consciousness,' I suggested. 'Walk a bit closer to the water and feel the water.'

Marie dropped the stone she was fiddling with and together, we walked to the water. We both put our hands in the water.

'The water is very cold,' Marie noticed.

'How about hearing the running water?'

'I was not aware of the sound of the water as I was focusing on my hands. But now that you mention it, I hear the streaming water,' she replied. 'Also, now that I am listening to the sound of the water, I was not so much aware of how cold the water is on my hands.'

'When I asked you to put your hands in the water, this sensory information was captured by the skin of your hands. This information was sent to the thalamus. The thalamus decided this information was relevant and sent it to the relevant parts of the cortex for processing.'

'And this is the moment that my brain told me that the water was cold?'

'Yes. As you were strongly focused on your hands, the sound that was captured by your ears was not regarded as very relevant. As a result, you were not consciously aware of the sound of the river.'

'And when I started to focus on the sound of the river, I was not aware of the cold water on my hands. I understand,' Marie concluded.

MARIE DRIED her hands by waving them around.

'As you've noticed, our brain does not consciously process all the information that is captured by our senses. But there is also one other important message here,' I told her. 'We can partly decide what we process consciously by directing our attention. We can decide to bring our full awareness to what we see or what we hear. We can also decide to close our eyes and to bring our full awareness to our touch sensation,' I continued. 'Although we tested this for our senses, we can also decide which thoughts we give our attention to. You remember that our thoughts are produced by our monkey mind, right?'

'Yes, thoughts about ourselves, others, the past and the future,' Marie added.

'Well remembered, Marie. Also here, to a certain extent we can decide which thoughts we activate,' I replied. 'Let me give you an example. I will tell you a short story and I want you to listen to my story as if you were interested in renting a holiday house. Are you ready?'

'Yes, I want a holiday house,' she smiled

I took a moment to reflect before I started telling the story.

'The holiday house I will describe to you is called 'the Corner Cottage'. This luxurious house is located on the top of a hill with an endless view over a valley. Reaching the house, the keys can be found in a key box on the right of the front door. You will enter into a large foyer where you can leave your shoes, coats, handbags and car keys. On the ground floor, you can find a spacious living-dining-kitchen area. Through the kitchen area, you have access to a covered porch. Enjoy the fresh air coming in by leaving the wide sliding doors open. The living area is decorated with beautiful paintings and art from the 19th century. The ground floor also has a master bedroom with a king-size bed and an en suite bath. The bath has a large window that can be left open to let some air in. Apart from the bathroom, all rooms on the ground floor have wooden walnut floors. Through the living area, you have free access to the garage that has space for two cars. The house is built on five acres and extremely private. There are no neighbours in close proximity. In the large garden, you will find a variety of trees, such as apple trees, pear trees, walnut trees and raspberry plants. Feel free to serve yourself! In the large shed in the garden, you can find a ping-pong table and four brand new e-bikes that you can use to explore the area. Beware that the shed can become very hot during the summer and we recommend leaving the side window open during the night to cool down. Last but not least, you will find a swimming pool at the back of the garden. The swimming pool is out of sight from the house so you take a walk to discover the area when you arrive. On the second level, you will find four large bedrooms and two bathrooms. All major rooms enjoy panoramic mountain views,' I enthusiastically described. 'I could go on for much longer. What do you think?'

'Waw, I would definitely want to stay in that house! The house seems to be huge and there seems to be an amazing mountain view. I love to pick fruit from trees and I cannot wait to jump in the swimming pool. How is your story related to us activating particular thoughts of our monkey mind?'

'I told you that we can partly decide which thoughts we consciously give our attention to. By telling you that you had to listen to my story as if you were interested in renting a holiday house, you activated a certain part of your network of thoughts,' I said. 'This is what you call taking a particular perspective. Your monkey mind has an idea about what you like and what you find important when you search for a holiday house.'

'So my monkey was searching for information that fits my role as a holiday house seeker!'

'That is exactly what your monkey was looking for. When I mentioned the swimming pool, your monkey called out "Waw, I want that!". A similar thing happened when I mentioned the large size of the house or the fruit trees. My monkey would have cheered by knowing there are e-bikes. The fact that there are no neighbours would have definitely made my monkey jump for joy,' I continued. 'We all have unique brains and will therefore hear and see different things, even though the exact same story is told to us,' I continued.

'Aha, so granny probably would have remembered the large garden so she can bring her dog,' Marie said.

I smiled. 'That is correct. Coming back now to steering our attention throughout the network of thoughts, I want you to think about my description of the holiday house as if you were a burglar. Can you do that?'

Marie nodded and reflected a while.

'What did your monkey tell you this time?' I asked her.

'I am not sure if I remember everything so well now. I don't think my monkey would have cheered when hearing about the swimming pool or the fruit trees. I am sure the monkey in my mind would have pointed out the expensive art and paintings.' She was quiet for a while. 'I guess that brand new e-bikes would have also excited my monkey.'

'Yes, and there were a few details in my story that a burglar most certainly would have noticed.'

We remained silent for a few moments.

'If I were a burglar, my monkey would have strongly pointed out the open window in the bathroom on the ground floor or the free access between the living area and the garage. Also, if the shed in the garden is aired during the night, this would offer me a way in to get to the brand new e-bikes. Not to forget that there are no neighbours around to alarm the police!'

'Waw, mama. These are details I really did not pay attention to!'

'I can imagine,' I replied. 'This is exactly what I mean with steering our attention to activate the thoughts that we want to activate. If we believe we are looking for a holiday house, the thoughts that are relevant for the search will be activated. If you were to listen to the description as a very old person, you might remember that there is a bedroom on the ground floor and you do not have to walk up the stairs every evening. The perspective we take will make us remember certain information and will filter out information that is irrelevant for our perspective.'

'This is why pregnant women see babies or prams everywhere, whereas they had not noticed so many before,' I added.

'And this is why I see food everywhere when I am hungry,' Marie smiled.

I remained silent for a minute to let Marie take in my words.

'But we are no burglars, nor are we searching for a holiday house,' Marie wondered out loud. 'How does that relate to my daily life?'

I smiled.

'Problem talk leads to problems. Solution talk leads to solutions.' I poked Marie in her side. She jumped up and laughed.

'PROBLEM TALK LEADS TO PROBLEMS. Solution talk leads to solutions,' Marie repeated.

'If we approach a challenging situation thinking of all the things that will be difficult, what will I hear, see and remember?' I challenged her.

'I get it. You will see, hear and remember all the things that will be difficult!'

'And if we approach a situation thinking of all the things that will run well?'

'... we will see, hear and remember all the things that will run well!' Marie completed my sentence.

'I do not want to say that we have to ignore potential problems in a situation. But assuming a situation will be problematic even before the problems have occurred is not necessarily helpful. The activation of the potential problems in your brain will activate the associated negative feelings.

These feelings will drain your mental energy even before these problems have occurred!'

We re-started our walk towards the Monastic site of Glendalough. The first part of our hike came closer to an ending.

'Think about the relationships that we have with others. The thoughts that are connected to the people in our life can have a very powerful influence on the quality of these relationships,' I said. 'Let me give you an example. We all know people we do not like that much. A long time ago, I worked together with a person I really did not like. I had several negative experiences with that person.'

'What type of negative experiences?'

'There was a strong clash between our personalities. I thought she was a very loud person and not always behaved in a fair way. Let me give you an example. During several meetings, when I was presenting a joint project, she interrupted me and finished the presentation. To make things worse, she was the one claiming all the appreciation for the work we actually both did'. 'So in my brain, that person became connected with negative thoughts and unpleasant feelings. At some point, even just thinking about that person gave me a bad feeling. Also, when I received an e-mail from her, I already felt stressed just seeing her name. My monkey was on alert "how will she annoy me this time?!". It is exactly with this perspective that I opened the e-mail and of course, what did I see, read and remember?'

'You saw and remembered the things that annoyed you,' Marie replied. 'So what did you do?'

'At some point, our working relationship ended because she took on a new job and moved to another city,' I replied. 'But you know what is funny? Years later I met her again on the street one day and we had this most lovely and heartwarming conversation. I do remember wondering why I never noticed that she is actually very witty.'

Marie winked at me. 'Well, that is because you took the perspective of the burglar and not of the holiday house seeker.'

I laughed.

'You are so right. I am not sure if you remember, but we talked about this situation once when you were still very young.'

'I don't remember that,' Marie replied.

'Well, you were still very young. You were only about four years old and I had picked you up from kindergarten. We were walking home and you looked at me. At a certain moment you asked: "Mama, what is wrong?". I asked you why you wondered. "Your face looks very grumpy," you replied. I was thinking about that lady from work on our walk home so I said: "I was just thinking of a lady from work that I don't like". You asked why I didn't like that lady. I tried to reply in a simple way and said: "This lady at work told me I didn't do my work well." Straight away you replied in this surprised and loving way: "But mama, you always do your work well!". "Hence the grumpy face, my love!" I shrugged. You remained quiet for some time and then suddenly said: "Mama, why don't you just think of a person you like.".'

Marie chuckled. 'I don't remember that.'

'Well I remember this very well. It made me laugh and most certainly pulled me out of my negative mood. Just think of a person you like, simple as that was your solution.'

I STOPPED WALKING and we both drank some water.

'But that also means that just thinking about negative events will lead to negative feelings? Or that thinking about positive events or people can lead to positive feelings,' Marie suggested.

'In our complex network of thoughts, certain thoughts are connected with negative feelings, certain thoughts are connected with positive feelings and certain thoughts might not be connected to a feeling at all,' I explained. 'We all know people we are not very fond of. Just thinking about that person can make you feel agitated. Luckily, we can also create a happy or cheerful feeling by thinking about a person we love or by simply activating a positive memory. Activating a memory can also mean re-living the associated feelings. Do you want to try it out?'

'Sure, why not.'

'Let's stand still for a moment and now close your eyes. Think back to the moment you crossed the finish line and won that 800 meter race. Can you picture it?'

'I can.' A smile appeared on Marie's face.

'How do you feel?' I asked.

She reflected.

'I feel proud and... I feel like I have wings. It makes me feel energized.'

Marie opened her eyes again.

'You see, just thinking about events that are connected with a positive feeling can allow us to re-live that feeling. The feelings were probably not as strong as they were the day of the event, but you did notice them, didn't you?'

'Oh yes. I am suddenly looking forward to my next training!' she enthusiastically replied.

'As I mentioned before, Marie: our thoughts can lead to our feelings. If you can master your thoughts, you are the master of your feelings,' I added. I took a moment to catch my breath.

'And these feelings contribute to the quality of our daily life and eventually our destiny.'

'But how do I master my thoughts?' Marie asked.

'We'll get there soon, Marie.'

WE COULD SEE the monastic site at this moment and it made me happy to think of soon being able to rest my shoulders, legs and feet. Just another 30 minutes of walking and we would reach the pub where we would have our evening dinner. Marie picked up a small stone and put it in her pocket. Ever since she was a child, she has been a stone collector.

'You know, mama,' she suddenly said, 'sometimes I wish I could just shut out my thoughts. If I feel stressed or I worry about something, I am not sure if thinking about a happy memory will help. Can't I just shut up the monkey in my mind so I will stop worrying and experience peace in my mind?'

I smiled. It is a question that I had asked myself several times a long time ago. The mental reset button. The way to serenity.

'I like that question,' I told her. 'Before I tell you how we can shut up the monkey in our mind, let me finally tell you how emotions can help us remembering events.'

'I had forgotten about that question,' Marie confessed.

'Well, we took a large detour, I must say. So where were we?'

'You told me about the part of the brain that decides

which information is sent to the cortex and which information is filtered out,' she remembered.

'Ah yes. The thalamus. As I mentioned, underneath the cortex, there is the limbic system, which plays an important role in our emotional life. The thalamus, the sensory relay station of the brain receives the information that is captured by our senses. This is what we see, hear, feel, taste and smell. You have understood now that the selection process of the thalamus decides what we process and which sensory information is filtered out. Also, we know that we can deliberately steer our attention to our different senses. If we bring our attention to our ears, we will be more aware of sounds. When we bring our attention to our eyes, we will be more aware of what we see. Most of the time, these processes run automatically and we process whatever the thalamus decides is relevant. However, because we can actively steer our attention to particular senses, we can therefore influence our sensory experiences.'

'And our feelings?'

'Yes, given that we construct our own feelings, this implies that we can influence them. At least, to a certain extent. As we tried out, the perspective we take can play an important role here. If we search for good things, it is more likely that the brain will consciously process good things. If we focus on the negative side of life, it is more likely that the brain will process and remember the negative side of life. Certain feelings, however, will just pop up and we cannot avoid experiencing them. Nevertheless, we can influence the intensity and power with which they influence our mind and behaviour. Before I explain this in more detail, let me tell you more about the other structures of the limbic system,' I suggested. 'Another part of the limbic system is the hypothalamus. The hypothalamus regulates the bodily functions that are part of our emotional life.'

'Bodily functions? I don't understand,' Marie interrupted.

'You told me that right before running your race, you felt a bit nervous, right? How did you know that you felt nervous?'

Marie frowned her eyes and was silent for a moment.

'Well of course I knew I was going to run an important race and just thinking about it before we started made me nervous.'

'So it was the thinking of the race that made you feel nervous. How did your body react?'

'I remember my heart was racing. I was also sweating a little and my stomach felt a little strange. I did not have a large appetite before the race,' Marie remembered.

'An emotion is a complex matter. Our thoughts or our personal interpretation of an event triggers a feeling of nervousness in this case. This feeling is associated with bodily changes, such as an acceleration of your heart rate, the slowing down or even stopping of your digestion system, which is why you lost your appetite when you felt nervous. Your sweat glands will increase sweat production and your mouth usually becomes dry. Some people become very pale or the contrary, they start flushing. It is those bodily functions that are regulated by the hypothalamus.'

Marie took a deep breath. 'Is that not strange? Why does the body react so strongly? In the end, it's just a race.'

'Well in pre-historic times, people often encountered real danger,' I said. 'To protect their own life, those strong bodily changes were essential.'

'Real dangers such as wild animals?'

'Yes, wild animals were a real danger to people. From the

moment a wild animal was spotted, the brain very quickly activated a fight-flight-freeze response. This is a reaction that helps us survive as humankind. We either fight the animal, we flee the situations as in "run for your life" or we freeze to hide from the animal. In order to fight or flee, our brain quickly prepares our body by increasing our heart rate, slowing down our digestion and increasing our sweat production. Slowing down our digestion allowes our body to save energy for the fight or flight. Also, the blood flow is diverted from our digestion to our muscles so that they are prepared to fight or flee. Increasing sweat production makes our skin more flexible and less prone to injuries. Especially the hands become sweatier, which also prevents overheating of the body. Typically, the pupils of our eyes dilate, which results in the so-called tunnel vision. This tunnel vision allows us to focus on the danger at hand. So all these bodily changes are necessary to actually fight or flee. They are the reason why we humans are still here today.'

'BUT WHY DID I feel those changes in my body before my race? This not a dangerous situation,' Marie reflected.

'It is not a real danger to you but your monkey mind interpreted the race as something really important, something where you were strongly challenged. This interpretation activated the amygdala in your brain and as a result, you experienced certain bodily changes. This is why your heart rate accelerated and your digestive system slowed down, for example,' I explained. 'By recognizing the situation as not a real danger, you were able to partly reduce that stress response.'

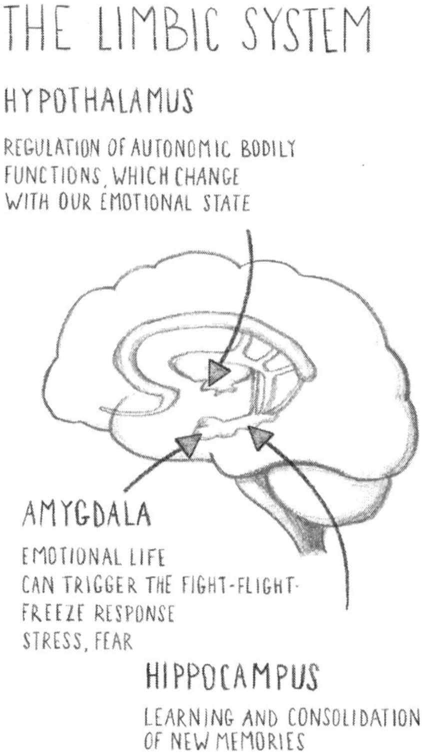

'The amygdala?' Marie asked. 'What is that?'

'The amygdala is another structure of the limbic system,' I explained. 'The amygdala triggers an emotion when we experience something that is emotionally relevant to us. Related to your question about remembering emotional events: the amygdala plays a crucial role in the formation of emotional memories,' I continued.

'Such as remembering the school play?' Marie suggested.

. . .

'THAT IS A GOOD EXAMPLE, yes. The reason why we remember emotional events better is because the amygdala closely cooperates with a structure that is important for memory formation, the hippocampus,' I said.

'I'm not sure if I can remember all the structures, mama!' Marie interrupted.

'There is no need to remember the structures by name. You will remember what is important to you while simply listening carefully,' I replied. 'The hippocampus plays an essential role in learning and the formation of memories. Hippocampus is the Greek word for seahorse. This part of the brain was called as such due to its resemblance to the structure of a seahorse. If you take a look at the limbic system, you can see that the amygdala and hippocampus are adjacent to each other. If the amygdala is triggered by an event, such as for example being on stage during a play, the brain tells us that this is an emotionally relevant event for us. The activation in the amygdala can activate the hippocampus, which helps in memorizing the event,' I explained.

'And that is why I remember emotional events better,' Marie said.

'Especially the formation of fear memories is guided by a close cooperation between the amygdala and hippocampus,' I added.

'Such as fear of snakes or wild animals?' Marie suggested.

'The amygdala plays an important role in all emotional events but especially in fear and stress emotions. Let's say you are walking through a forest and suddenly you hear a sizzling sound in the bushes. You slow down your walking pace and before you realize it, a snake approaches you and bites you in the leg. What will happen? Your amygdala becomes active before you are able to reflect on the situation and your body quickly comes into a fight-flight-freeze state. You probably run away.

Importantly, the hippocampus was triggered strongly, which resulted in a strong emotional memory of the event. In your brain, a snake became connected with very strong amygdala activation. As a result, you developed a very strong fear of snakes. And how long did it take your brain to learn this?' I asked her.

'A few seconds?'

'If even that long. When such experiences are accompanied by strong amygdala and hippocampus activation, they could lead to a phobia,' I told her. 'We have learnt the hard way that snakes are dangerous. In our brain, the snake is connected with strong amygdala activation. A phobia can be so bad that the monkey starts panicking when you only just think of a snake. The monkey starts yelling and screaming in your mind. The entire fight-flight-freeze reaction might be activated simply by thinking of a snake. You might start sweating, have a strange feeling in your stomach or your heart rate accelerates.'

Marie reflected.

'I can't wait to understand how we can just shut out our thoughts,' she said. 'It seems that our thoughts really have a lot of power over our feelings and life quality. Sometimes it feels more like a zoo than a monkey in my mind.'

I smiled.

We had arrived at the monastic site where again we met the lady with the green hat.

'It seems we are taking the same route today?'

I smiled at her while Marie greeted the lady.

The lady smiled back.

'It is such great weather. I packed so many warm and waterproof clothes as I thought it rains at least five times a day in Ireland,' the lady laughed and continued her walk. We waved her goodbye.

The weather was indeed lovely and we sat on the grass. I felt light after taking off my backpack and I took off my shoes. I let the grass touch my feet and took a deep breath. Marie followed my example.

'The grass feels so nice,' Marie smiled and began performing cartwheels. 'Can you do cartwheels, mama?'

'Don't challenge me, Marie,' I replied with a smile.

'Come and join me!'

I noticed my monkey mind silently call out: "Are you not too old?" or "Are there not too many people watching?" or "Can you even still do a cartwheel?" even though deep down I was wondering how great it would be to try out a cartwheel. Marie's cheers were just too contagious. I stood up, took a little run and performed a cartwheel.

'Not bad!' Marie giggled. 'Just straighten your legs a little bit more'.

I performed another cartwheel. It was one of many cartwheels that late afternoon next to the monastic site of Glendalough.

My monkey cheered.

DAY 2

Glendalough - Roundwood

'I'm not sure if I can finish this omelette,' I said staring at the huge plate in front of me. 'This is one fat omelette.'

'Probably from a fat chicken,' Marie joked.

After a good night of rest, Marie and I were sitting at the breakfast table of our Bed & Breakfast. After our round of cartwheels on the grass, we had a great meal at the local pub of Laragh, followed by an early night. The long hike, the cartwheels and the fresh air had resulted in a sound and deep sleep.

Today's hiking day would lead us to Roundwood over the Scarr Mountain. A good walk for which a strong Irish breakfast was the best preparation, I thought when looking at my omelette.

'Do you have any questions for me today, young lady?' I asked Marie as we started our walk.

'Well you told me about the monkey mind. You also explained to me that underneath the cortex, there is the limbic system. The limbic system plays an important role in our emotional life and memory formation. Oh, and of course we talked about Vanessa who was stuck in a life she did not like but who is travelling the world as we speak,' Marie remembered well.

She remained silent for a moment.

'I know now that my thoughts play an important role in my emotions,' Marie continued. 'But how can we influence our thoughts and emotions?'

I took a moment to reflect.

'It is our power to influence our thoughts and emotions that eventually allows us to become the best version of ourselves,' I said out loud. 'Let me tell you more about what potential and performance means.'

We slowed down our pace as we started walking up Paddock Hill, which would bring us to the foot of Scarr Mountain.

'The way that I look at performance, is that it stands for your potential minus your internal interferences. The performance is what you and other people can observe. For example, you running a race in a certain time, holding a presentation, writing a report or working out creative ideas. The potential that you have refers to your talents, your skills, your know-how, your expertise, your experiences and so forth. In the best case, your performance reflects the potential that you have. We all have potential and this is unique for each person. Do you have any idea what comprises your potential?'

Marie thought about the question.

'I am good at running and tennis. I easily learn a new language and I think I sing quite well,' Marie said.

'Indeed, these are examples of your potential. This potential is yours and nobody can take this away from you. Remember I told you that nobody can take away your potential to run that 800 meter race very well?'

Marie nodded.

'Unfortunately, in many situations we do not have full access to our potential because we are dealing with so-called internal interferences or blockages.'

'What are those?'

'Let me explain this to you with an example. I know you have a great potential to sing. You have a certain talent to sing and you have a weekly practice in the choir. Imagine that you are alone at home and you are singing when you are alone in the kitchen. You bring your best performance. Your full potential to sing is brought out.'

Marie smiled.

'Now imagine the next day, you are at a party and someone hears you are singing in a choir. That person asks you to stand up and sing a song for all the people at the party. What will happen?'

'I hope this will never happen,' Marie quickly responded. 'I am quite sure that I will not bring my best performance. In fact, I might not sing well at all!'

'Did you lose your potential to sing? Did you leave it at home?'

'No, of course not.' Marie smiled.

'Then what happened?'

'I guess I became nervous. I felt a bit put on the spot and I was afraid other people might laugh. I felt under pressure and very stressed,' Marie continued.

'Exactly. Your monkey mind started to tell you a story. It told you that you were under pressure and that people might laugh. It is the inner voice, the monkey mind that suddenly caused internal interferences or blockages.'

'And it is those interferences that blocked me in my potential to sing,' Marie concluded. 'So what can I do?'

'I told you that performance stands for the potential that you have minus the internal interferences, right? Well, increasing performance in a healthy and natural way means bringing out the potential that you have here and now, and requires you to reduce the internal blockages. The skill that allows us to reduce those blockages is called self-regulation.'

'SELF-REGULATION?' Marie looked at me puzzled.

'Self-regulation is our capacity to recognize and down-regulate our internal blockages. As such, it allows us to unlock our potential and so eventually become the best version of ourselves. Or put differently, self-regulation allows us to unlock our potential and bring it into performance to the extent it is possible.'

'Can I improve my self-regulation?'

'Self-regulation is a personality trait, meaning that we are all born with a certain level of self-regulation strength. But, luckily it is also a skill that we can improve,' I explained. 'Self-regulation has received a lot of attention in research. The interest in studying self-regulation got an enormous boost when Professor Walter Mischel conducted the Marshmallow experiment in the seventies at Stanford University.'

'Marshmallow as in those soft, spongy sweet things that we sometimes melt on the fire after barbecue?' Marie asked.

'Exactly those. I once did the marshmallow experiment with you when you were three years old, do you remember?'

Marie gave me a confused expression.

'Well, let me explain to you how this experiment works. This experiment is usually conducted with young children, between the ages of 4 and 7 years old. The child is asked to sit at a table. On the table is a small plate with one marshmallow. The researcher tells the child that if the child does not eat the marshmallow while he is out of the room until his return, the child would receive another marshmallow.

After explaining the deal, the researcher leaves the room for about 15 minutes.'

'Oh jee. That is a mean experiment! That means that the children have to choose between a small reward right now or a bigger one later on.'

'This is indeed not an easy task for a young child. Interestingly, those children were followed over a longer life span. Walter Mischel and his team found that those children who were able to wait longer in front of the marshmallow while the researcher was absent had better academic grades, better career chances and a healthier lifestyle as an adult. More studies confirmed these results: children with stronger self-regulation strength tend to have more success in life, both privately and professionally. However, a recent study that tried to replicate those results had to conclude that not only self-regulation but also the economic background plays a significant role in success in life. Nevertheless, self-regulation is a vital strength for the quality of life.'

'So how did I perform when I did the test?'

I smiled.

'I did not use a marshmallow but bread sticks, crissini's. As a child you loved those.'

'Yes, I remember crissini's!'

'I had given you a crissini and told you not to eat it yet. Louise was still a baby and I was preparing the pram to take you two out for a walk. I told you that if you would wait until we were all set and outside the house, I would give you another one.'

'So what did I do?'

'Very calmly you waited for all of us to be ready for our walk. Once outside, I gave you a second crissini. I was very distracted because Louise was crying in the pram and did not want to settle. Due to my distraction, I only noticed halfway through our walk that you were still holding the two crissini's in your tiny hands.'

'Mama!' Marie laughed out loud.

I joined her laughing and said: 'Don't worry, I told you straight away you were allowed to eat them and so you happily did.'

'How about Louise? Did you also do the experiment with her?'

'Oh, I tried, ...' I smiled thinking back at the moment we were sitting at the table.

'The crissini was eaten before I had finished explaining the deal!'

Marie smiled.

WE HAD ARRIVED at the foot of the Scarr Mountain. The sun was out and the landscapes around us appeared fresh and green. Marie stretched out her arms and joyfully started her climb of the mountain. Her body language spoke of pure serenity and happiness.

'Does that mean that Louise will not have much success in life because she ate the crissini without waiting for the second one?'

I started to laugh. 'No, absolutely not. First of all, I did not set up a controlled experiment to actually test this and it was also me, as her mum, giving her a crissini. But even if she would have eaten the marshmallow in a real experiment, I would not worry.'

'But did you not just tell me that children who were able to wait longer had more success in life?'

'I did say that indeed. But this is only a small part of the full story. I told you that self-regulation exists as a personality trait, right? This implies that all people are born with a particular level of self-regulation strength. Some people can regulate themselves naturally very well, others find it more challenging to self-regulate. Everyone is somewhere on the scale. But remember, self-regulation is also a skill that we can train and improve.'

'How can we improve our self-regulation?' Marie asked.

'To understand how we can improve our self-regulation, let's have another look at how the brain works,' I suggested. 'Most of the internal interferences that block us in our potential are caused by too much activation in the emotional system of our brain, where the amygdala plays a major role. Although we need the amygdala for our physical survival, for our emotional life and the formation of emotional memories, intense negative thoughts and feelings can block us in our potential. Strong amygdala activation is related to feelings of stress and anxiety in situations where there is no real danger.'

'Such as just thinking of a snake or standing on stage?'

'Yes, also stage fright is a good example. There is no real danger standing on a stage to give a presentation or to sing a song. Nevertheless, the monkey mind tells us, often without us being conscious of the message, that "we do not want to fail in the presence of others" or "that we are simply not good enough", ... The fear of social embarrassment is a very strong interference. The monkey voice might trigger the amygdala and you know the rest of the story.'

'Our body will be prepared for fight, flight or freeze. We start sweating, feel queasy in our stomach and might even start shaking,' Marie completed the description.

'Sometimes the stress reaction might be so strong that people even experience loss of memory or forget the lyrics of their song,' I continued.

'How does that happen?'

'Well, for many of the tasks that are an expression of our potential, we need a completely different part of the brain. It is the frontal part of the brain that is called the prefrontal cortex. It is the prefrontal cortex that plays an important role in our executive functions. This part of the brain plays an essential role in planning and organizing our behaviour, reaching our goals, using our working memory, thinking of solutions, making well thought out decisions or setting priorities. These are just a few examples. In fact, many of the tasks that we mentally engage in during the day require an involvement of the prefrontal cortex,' I continued. 'Now think back to the example where you were walking in a forest and you were bitten by a snake. Recognizing the snake instantly activated the amygdala, which in turn rapidly triggered the fight-flight-freeze response.'

'Without really thinking, right?' Marie added.

'In fact, you were not capable of thinking. In this case, the expression "think or survive" kicks in. If you were able to take time to reflect, you would have endangered your life. The quick fight-flight-freeze response even shuts out the prefrontal cortex. As a result, you will not think or reflect but as quickly as possible bring yourself to safety through fighting, running or hiding,' I explained.

'And also in situations where the amygdala is triggered strongly without the presence of a real danger, the prefrontal cortex will be put out of play so to say,' Marie concluded.

'The amygdala and the prefrontal cortex are very closely connected. As a result, they can easily influence each other.

This connection, as we just discussed, allows the amygdala to put the prefrontal cortex out of play when there is a real danger. It helps in our survival. But as you correctly mentioned, a similar pattern of activation can emerge when the amygdala is triggered without a real danger.'

'So when I went on stage for that school play, my amygdala became active and my prefrontal cortex was shut off?'

'In case of real danger, the amygdala will be strongly triggered and the prefrontal cortex will be put out of play. However, when there is no real danger and the amygdala is triggered, your capacity to think and reflect will likely deteriorate. Furthermore, the prefrontal cortex will work to reduce the amygdala activation as the brain recognizes that there is no real danger, using even more energy. And now the bad news comes,' I continued.

'Do I really want to know?' Marie laughed.

'Well, it will certainly put certain life events in perspective,' I smiled. 'The bad news is that the prefrontal cortex has a limited capacity.'

'Do you mean like a battery?'

'Yes, similar to a mental battery. Although the workings of the prefrontal cortex in reality are much more complex, we could us the metaphor of a battery here. When our mental battery is fully charged, we have a lot of energy at our disposal to deal with stress, like the excessive amygdala activation, and to deal with all those tasks in which the prefrontal cortex plays an important role. However, the more you use the mental battery, the more it will be empty and the more challenging all your daily tasks will be.'

I SMILED and had to think back to a few examples of days where I reached the limits of my mental battery more than once.

'Let me give you another metaphor of how the activation level in the amygdala and prefrontal cortex fluctuates during a challenging work day. Keep in the back of your mind that for a good mental balance and performance, we want the mental battery to be fully charged. In addition, as long as there is no real danger, we want the amygdala not to be too activated so that we do not experience too much stress. I will give you a description of a normal working day that I had when you and Louise were still very little,' I suggested.

'That sounds fun,' Marie smiled.

'Louise was not an easy sleeper as a baby. Because I got up several times during the night, most of the mornings I woke up with a lack of sleep. When we suffer from a lack of sleep, our mental battery is not fully charged. I got out of bed and got both of you ready for school. While I was dressing Louise, you decided to put on your summer dress. But it was snowing outside! You were very stubborn and refused to take off your summer dress. So what did I do? I tried to calmly negotiate you into trousers, which required a lot of energy from my mental battery. At the same time the clock was ticking and I was expected at work. Having put on trousers underneath your dress, we were finally in the car. You were screaming in the car because you were wearing trousers while I was scratching the ice off the car windshield. After a tearful and loud drive to the kindergarten, I was finally on my way to work. When I arrived at work, I had already used half of my mental battery and I felt an increase in my stress levels. There is no point in describing all the tasks I had to do at work. I was still working as a scientist at that point and most of my daily tasks required a lot of cognitive work. To summarize my day at the office, I can tell you I had used most of my mental battery by the time I picked the two of you up from kindergarten. I had promised to take you and Louise swimming for the first time. I had secretly hoped you had forgotten about this plan but no, this was the first thing that you mentioned when I picked you up from kindergarten. Once we arrived at the swimming pool, I noticed I was simply running on autopilot and had very little mental energy left. When we were in the changing room taking off all the warm layers of winter clothing, I noticed that I had forgotten Louise's swimming nappy. There was no way I was going to tell you that swimming was off. It was our first time swimming. I decided to give Louise a fresh, normal nappy and put on her swimming wings. Once Louise was ready, I helped you with your swimsuit and with inflating your swimming wings. When we were both ready, I turned around to find out that Louise was not in the changing room anymore. She had left us by crawling through the gap that was at the bottom of the door!'

'Oh no, mama!' Marie started to laugh. I could not help but join in and said: 'I can laugh at the situation now, looking back and knowing all was fine in the end. But at that moment, my stress levels were spiking and I am not sure if I had any mental battery left at all!'

'Where was Louise?'

'She was not far. She was hopping up and down a bit further outside in the hall.'

'Well, I can tell you now that wearing a normal nappy in a swimming pool is NOT a great idea! That day, I learnt how much fluid a nappy can suck up. Louise's nappy pretty much ballooned from the moment we went into the water!' I could not help but laugh by mentally activating the image of that moment.

'Oh, mama, that is embarrassing!' Marie joined me in giggling heartily.

'Marie, I was completely worn out. I was absolutely depleted.'

~

'WHAT DOES that mean "to be depleted"?' Marie curiously asked.

'Let's take a break first,' I suggested.

We had arrived at the top of Scarr Mountain and I took a moment to catch my breath. From the top of Scarr Mountain, we had a 360° panoramic view of the Wicklow Mountains. The view was simply breathtaking and gave me an instant feeling of happiness. Marie also became very quiet and started to spin around stretching her arms sideways. The sun was out and looking into the direction of Bray, we could see the Irish sea shimmering in the Sun. We could see how the landscape below us was divided into fields, separated by tree lines. Houses appeared so tiny, like toys we could pick up. I pulled Marie close and kissed her on her forehead. From the expression on her face, I could see how present and relaxed she was.

'Oh hello again,' a voice with a strong Spanish accent broke the silence. 'It seems that also today we are walking the same path.'

The lady with the green hat was eating a sandwich. 'By the way, my name is Cristina,' she stretched out her hand.

'I am Marie,' Marie shook her hand.

'Nice to meet you, Cristina. My name is Juliet, I am Marie's mother,' I said while shaking her hand.

'Do you mind if we join you?' I asked, pointing at the stone she was sitting on.

'Not at all, please take a seat. The view is absolutely stunning,' Cristina warmly mentioned.

Marie and I sat down next to Cristina and took out our lunches.

'Is this the first time you are hiking the Wicklow Way?' I asked Cristina.

'It is the first time that I am hiking the Wicklow Way, indeed. I have, however, hiked several pilgrim routes before. Four years ago, I hiked a part of the Camino de Santiago,' Cristina responded.

'Where is the Camino de Santiago?' Marie wondered out loud.

Cristina drew a map with her index finger on a stone.

'If this image represents Spain, then Santiago de Compostella is a city about here in the northwest of Spain. It is relatively close to the border with Portugal. There are many pilgrim routes that you can walk to Santiago de Compostella. I hiked the most popular route, which starts in France in a village called "Jean Pied de Port".'

Marie made big eyes. 'Wow, so you walked all the way from France to Spain! How long did it take you?'

'Well,' Cristina reflected, 'I took me a little bit more than 5 weeks. I walked between 24 and 27 kilometres per day and I took a few days off.'

'That is a very long walk,' Marie replied.

It seems Cristina was a little lost in her own thoughts.

'It was a time when hiking was the only thing I was still able to do,' she eventually said.

'What do you mean?' Marie asked.

'I'm sorry to hear that, Cristina,' I quickly replied. 'We do not want to intrude.'

'You are not at all intruding,' Cristina smiled at Marie. 'I am happy to tell you more if you would like to know?'

'Well yes gladly, if you don't mind,' I replied.

CRISTINA TOOK a sip of water and started to tell her story.

'After finishing law school, I started to work at a prestigious law firm in Madrid. After studying for five years and living on a waitress wage, I enjoyed the financial freedom that came with the job. It soon turned out that the competition in the law firm was very tough. I had started working at the firm together with seven other junior lawyers who were all eager to make a career. I remember that on the first day of work, all junior lawyers were introduced to each other over a delicious breakfast. After living as a student for many years, the breakfast simply looked like a luxurious lifestyle. So I indulged,' Cristina laughed. 'The atmosphere during the breakfast was light, friendly and joyful. At least, that was until one of the partners of the firm entered the room. I will never ever forget what he said that morning. After introducing himself as one of the founders and partners of the firm, he said: "Look around. Look at the person on your right hand side. Look at the person on your left hand side. Look at the person in front of you. Only one of you is going to make it here. It could be you." With these words he confidently smiled and left the room. From being light and friendly, the atmosphere suddenly turned to confusion and eventually into a cold, hard competition among the junior lawyers.'

'Did you make it?' Marie asked Cristina.

Cristina laughed. 'Well, Marie. I suppose the answer depends on your definition of "making it". I felt a large conflict between cooperation and self-promotion. On the one hand, we were dependent on each other for most of the project work. On the other hand, to make it to the next career level, it means you had to be better than the rest. Or put differently, you do not necessarily have to be better than the rest but you need to be perceived as better than the rest. This means that it was important to attract big law cases. The lawyers who attracted big law cases were the ones bringing in the big money. Also, it was important to be recognized – even if it was not necessarily you who did all or most of the work. Most importantly, people had to think it was you. It was all about reputation, you see,' Cristina continued.

'That sounds like an exhausting situation,' I commented. 'How did you manage?'

'For a long time, I was not even aware of the fact that it was exhausting. Don't forget that I was still very young and full of energy. Also, I was and still am very passionate about the work itself. I was used to studying hard so I didn't mind working the extra hours. Quite often, I worked in the office until midnight and was back at my desk at 7am,' Cristina confessed.

'That must have been exhausting for your prefrontal cortex,' Marie stated.

'My prefrontal what?' Cristina asked.

Marie briefly explained to Cristina that we need the prefrontal cortex to engage in tasks that require executive functions, such as planning and organising our behaviour , making decisions and reaching our goals. She told Cristina that we use the metaphor of a mental battery to refer to the fact that our brain does not have unlimited resources for activities that require mental processing. The mental battery is not fully charged when we don't sleep enough and keeps using energy for mentally demanding tasks.

Cristina listened carefully.

'That makes a lot of sense,' Cristina nodded. 'I noticed that nights when I slept very little, I could not concentrate well the next day. After those nights, I felt I had this mental fog and was easily agitated. But my long hours of work paid off. I was promoted to the next career level after two years and won my first big cases. I started to earn a lot of money, which I spent on renting a luxurious apartment in one of the nicest areas of Madrid.'

'You must have really enjoyed such a luxurious apartment,' Marie said.

Cristina reflected.

'No, actually not,' she stated. 'Looking back, I believe I spent too little time in that place to really enjoy it. Although being able to rent this apartment in this prestigious area of Madrid helped me to keep going in my job. With this apartment, I had gained a certain status, I suppose. Also, I believed that I had earned it for my long hours of work. Somehow, I felt that I should receive good compensation for spending all my time, often including weekends, at the office. Coming back to your question, Marie, I don't think that this apartment made me happy. As I said, I was seldom there.'

'Was your job making you happy?' I wondered.

Cristina thought about it and then said: 'I am ashamed to tell you that my job did not make me happy. I did enjoy the work itself as I was able to fight for causes that I truly believe in. But the entire mindset and competitive working environment that I worked in ruined it for me. I see that now. At the time, though, I did not take time to ponder the question whether I was happy or not. I was making a successful career. That was important. I worked hard and I received my reward in the sense of promotion and bonuses, that, however, I had no time to spend. Well, once a year I took a two-week vacation in an expensive resort. By the time I had fully arrived – body *and* mind at the holiday destination – and was able to relax, it was time to go back home. And so the story continued,' Cristina sadly said. 'There is no point in visiting the Himalayas if the Himalayas are not in your mind.'

I smiled.

'Taking a two-week vacation in an expensive resort does not make any sense when your monkey is not relaxed, right?' Marie said and winked at me.

Now Cristina looked puzzled. 'What monkey?'

'In our brain we have this monkey, a voice that is constantly chatting to us. This monkey mind produces our thoughts. These are thoughts about ourselves, about others, about our past and future. This monkey constantly chats and tells you what to think, how to feel and how to behave,' Marie explained to Cristina.

'You could also compare it with the hamster wheel of thoughts. Especially in times of stress, it seems impossible to slow down the hamster wheel. These are times when we worry a lot or when we cannot sleep because our thoughts or worries are keeping us awake,' I further explained to Cristina.

Cristina drank some water and thought about all this for a moment.

'Many experiences seem to fall into place after listening to what the two of you tell me and looking back at how I lived my life,' Cristina said. 'When I mentioned that it took me nearly two weeks to mentally arrive at my holiday destination or to mentally relax, it was indeed the hamster wheel of thoughts that was overactive. Wherever I was, the hamster wheel of thoughts kept me busy and stressed. I was stuck in my own head. Indeed, I could have been in the Himalayas without taking in the Himalayas. I would have been absorbed by my own thoughts rather than being present in the moment.'

~

'So if your job was not making you happy, what made you happy?' Marie asked.

'Well, let me tell you again that the work itself was often fulfilling me as I was able to fight for important causes that were in line with my deeper values. I believe it was the entire competitive context that made me work for the wrong reasons. At some point, it felt that I was not connected to my true values anymore. I was not true to myself and this made me unhappy. I was lost in a wrong definition of life success,' Cristina sighed deeply. 'But there was a moment that I did strongly connect with a feeling of great happiness. After ten years of working for the law firm, I fell in love, Marie.'

Cristina had caught our attention even more now.

'I was working on a pro bono case for a school that did not have the financial means to pay for a proper lawsuit. After having several cases of sick children, the school had found out that the caterer of the food for the canteen had regularly used expired meat. It was through my work with the school that I met Juan, a young teacher of my age. I still remember the sparkles with which he talked about his work with the kids. Each time we talked, I felt energized seeing the great passion for his work. And a passion for life in general. It was the kind of passion that was contagious and gave me energy. He really wanted to make a difference for the world around him. We fell in love and soon we were in a relationship,' Cristina continued.

I noticed a hint of sadness in her voice.

'At the beginning, we were mostly spending our weekends together because I was working my long hours during the week. When I arrived home from work, he was already asleep and most mornings, I left for work before breakfast. I remember how much I was looking forward to those weekends. The time together with Juan was the happiest time of my life,' Cristina said with a sparkle in her eyes.

'Did you get married?' Marie hopefully asked.

'Unfortunately not,' Cristina sighed. 'After we were in a relationship for a year, I took on a big case at work, which requested my presence at the weekends. At the start, Juan was very supportive. As you might guess, my level of stress, the long hours of work and the lack of time together drove us apart. We seldom saw each other and we often had heated arguments on the few occasions that we were together,' Cristina continued. 'Our relationship took a huge turn one day when I came home late from work. Juan was already asleep and had left a note on the kitchen table. I will never forget what was on the note – I will always keep it safe.'

'What did the note say?' I wondered.

'It was a playful little poem from Juan. It said:

Cristina, Cristina, Cristina, my beautiful love, my playful dove.

Allow our passion and love to write its own story
Let's live its natural happiness and glory.
I wish for you to be with me
Let us soon be filling life with three.'

'These are beautiful lines, Cristina.'

. . .

'Oh, they are,' Cristina continued. 'I still remember every detail of that evening. I had read the poem over and over again and deep down, I felt so happy. However, after a few moments, my monkey mind was telling me that having a baby would reduce my career chances. "How would you manage?" the monkey asked me. "You worked so hard to get here, are you willing to put that all at risk," my monkey called out. I remember that voice made me really sad and I felt I could not escape nor fight it. I went upstairs, kissed Juan while he was asleep and cried myself to sleep,' Cristina silently said with sadness in her voice.

'Why were you sad?' Marie carefully asked.

'Because I had decided to tell Juan the next day that the relationship was over.'

'Did you not want to start a family?' Marie asked.

Cristina gave Marie a kind and warm smile.

'Oh, Marie, there is nothing I wanted more than to start a family with Juan. I always wanted to have children, a daughter, like yourself. I am reminded of that wish even more now looking at you.'

'I am sorry to hear that. But then why did you break up with Juan?' Marie asked Cristina.

'I was blinded by my career obsession. Or perhaps it was the high level of stress that had separated me from myself. Remember I told you that the time I was together with Juan was pure happiness for me. I had never experienced such a beautiful feeling. When we were together, I did not want the moment to end. At the same time, the purity and greatness of that feeling made me insecure. As I understood now, it was my monkey mind telling me that "I should focus on work", that "my life was about making career" and "that only one of all the junior lawyers that started with me would make it to partner". Looking back, I wish I had had the courage not to listen to my monkey and act in line with my true values. I wish that instead I had listened to my heart,' Cristina said.

'Was there not a possibility to have both your job and your relationship with Juan?' Marie wondered out loud.

'Not with the work mindset and the competitive work environment that I lived in those days. I am sure there was a way to work it out, but you know, Marie, I was mentally exhausted. I had no mental energy left to break bad habits. I also noticed that my mental performance was going down and my stress levels were difficult to control,' Cristina sighed. 'Looking back, I wonder why Juan fell in love with me in the first place.'

~

I LOOKED AT MARIE.

'Do you remember I told you about depletion?' I checked with her.

'Depletion?' Cristina and Marie repeated in synchrony.

'I told you that our mental battery has a limited capacity, right?'

Cristina nodded.

'The prefrontal cortex is in very close connection with our amygdala. As I explained to Marie before, the amygdala is located deep inside our brain. Actually, there are two of them, one on the left hand side and one on the right hand side. Although the amygdala are very small, basically the shape and size of an almond, they play a powerful role in our life. The amygdala are mainly important for our survival, for triggering emotions and also for the formation of emotional memories, such as remembering the evening that you found that note, Cristina,' I continued.

'That was a very emotional evening, indeed. I remember many details of that night.'

'Although we need the amygdala, they are also involved in setting off stress reactions. Also, a heightened activation is connected to feelings of anxiety or depression,' I continued. 'Remember I told you that the prefrontal cortex is strongly connected to the amygdala. Because of this connection, the prefrontal cortex has the possibility to control the amygdala activation to a certain extent. Let me give you an example. We all have to deal with people we do not like much. When we have to spend time with such a person, our monkey mind will start talking to us about that person. The monkey might say things, such as "Is he doing it again?" or "I can't believe he is saying that!" and so on. Many times, we are not even consciously aware of this inner voice. This voice, however, interprets everything that the other person does in a negative way because in our mind, that person is connected with a negative emotion,' I continued.

'And it is this negative interpretation that will increase the amygdala activation,' Cristina suggested.

'And the increased amygdala activation will make us feel stressed,' Marie concluded.

'Indeed. So, first lesson: our thoughts can lead to our feelings. Second lesson: the increase in amygdala activation will lead to a stress reaction in our body and we will feel stressed or if it is really bad, mentally exhausted.'

'How again is the prefrontal cortex involved?' Cristina wanted to know.

'Well, if there is a real actual danger coming from outside, the amygdala will generate a strong trigger of our survival mode. As an example, we see a snake and we react with the typical fight, flight or freeze reaction. When this survival mode kicks in, it puts the prefrontal cortex out of play. If we would be able to calmly contemplate the situation, we might be dead already. So looking at this from an evolutionary point of view, it is essential for our survival that the prefrontal cortex is shut out in case of a real physical danger,' I explained.

'But the person we do not like is not a real danger,' Cristina commented.

'And yet meeting or even just thinking of that person can increase our stress levels. The point I want to come to is that when the amygdala is triggered and sets off a stress reaction even if there is no real danger to our life, the prefrontal cortex might try to reduce the amygdala activation,' I said.

'Do I understand correctly that the prefrontal cortex will use its resources to deal with my amygdala activation?' Cristina asked.

'Have you already noticed that those days when you felt stressed, you were more mentally exhausted in the evening compared to those days where you did a similar amount of work but without too much stress?' I asked Cristina.

'Most certainly. I remember that during my time at the law firm, I once worked on a fascinating case with my favourite colleague. Her name was Valeria. I loved to work with her. She was very funny, we laughed a lot at work. Also, she seemed genuinely kind and not interested in stabbing me in the back to advance her own career. Unfortunately, with this kind behaviour, it was impossible to make a career at my law firm. To answer your question, Juliet: working on a case I thought was fascinating, together with Valeria, did not mentally exhaust me that much. I also worked long hours, but there were many evenings I even still had energy left after I got home from a long day at work.'

'Stress is the largest energy killer,' I stated. 'When our mental battery is busy dealing with our stress, it uses up the limited resources very quickly. We more easily feel mentally exhausted and reach our limits.'

Both Cristina and Marie seemed to be lost in their own reflections as I took a break from talking to drink a bit of water and take a deep breath.

'So is that the meaning of depletion? Feeling mentally exhausted because you used up the energy in your mental battery?' Marie asked.

'It is. Unfortunately, we reach this state of depletion mostly at a time when we are expected to have the best time of our lives. That is, after a day of hard work when we are finally at home with our loved ones. During the day, we used most of our mental energy, the amygdala receives more free play and after a stressful day we end up behaving like a bad version of ourselves.'

'Looking back at how I felt,' Cristina said, 'this makes a lot of sense. The more years I worked for the law firm, the more I was obviously overusing my mental battery. On top of that, I was sleeping 5-6 hours a night, which made the mental exhaustion even worse.'

'What happened in the end? Did you become a partner?' I asked Cristina.

'No,' Cristina smiled, 'luckily not.'

'Why do you say luckily,' Marie quickly wanted to know. 'I thought you wanted to become a partner?'

'For a long time, I believed that was my goal in life. Let's say nature decided differently for me,' Cristina continued. 'When I had broken up with Juan, I started to work even more. I wanted to forget that I had been happy with Juan. Soon after, I started to notice the symptoms of my "depletion". I am sure that I had them much before I started to notice them but somehow, I had lost the connection with my own body,' Cristina explained to us.

'Stress separates us from ourselves,' I said. 'Which symptoms of depletion did you notice?'

'I could not escape my own thoughts. Especially during the night, it became so bad I hardly slept. The less I slept, the worse my condition became. My body became very shaky. I noticed how my hands started to tremble and my heart was racing. My back and muscles became very tense, which made my sleeping problems even worse. I guess that was the result of my overactive amygdala, right?'

'Yes, when we experience excessive levels of stress, we usually also start breathing more shallowly and get problems with our digestion. Most of us start experiencing more frequent colds and infections. This is not a surprise since stress can be a direct attack on our immune system. As a result, the immune system becomes weak and we more easily get ill,' I continued.

'Oh yes, I have seen all those symptoms. In all their intensity and shapes. Also mentally, I was suffering. I could not focus anymore, my memory was seriously failing me and I started to behave aggressively towards my colleagues. I was short with them and accused them of poor work when we did not win a case. At that moment, I had already become a senior lawyer and had my own team working for me. I am not proud to tell you, but I really was a bad person to work for. One day, it all got out of hand.'

'What happened?' Marie encouraged Cristina to tell us more.

'One day, I noticed a case file missing. As soon as I noticed, I got in such a rage and started to blame my team for doing such a poor job. I told them that if they did not do a better job, they should leave the firm. My team had seen me in a bad condition, but this was really the worse I had been. Tomas, one of my team members had the courage to suggest that maybe I should take some time off to rest. I had been ill for over two weeks but had not taken the time to recover. I admire Tomas for speaking up, but at the time his comment increased my rage even more. To spare you the details, I cursed so loudly that one of the partners had to intervene. The entire office, including visiting clients, had witnessed my rage. I had behaved not only unprofessionally but more importantly, I can see now, I had lost all and any sense of respect for other people,' Cristina said with an expression of shame on her face.

'I was caught in my own head with only one focus: myself.'

'I can see that this state of depletion makes you the worst version of yourself!' Marie commented.

~

We were silent for a moment, collecting our thoughts and impressions.

'Well in my case,' Cristina continued, 'I was far beyond depletion. The moment I got home, I wanted to fight the decision of being forced to take a leave. That fight took me about... 5 minutes. Soon, I gave in and I collapsed on my bed and started to sob. Quickly, the sobs turned into crying. I cried for a few hours, just lying there on the bed. The first thought that crossed my mind was: "My Goodness, Cristina, you have not even taken the time to cry properly the last fifteen years!". I cried for losing Juan, for the happiness I had lost by leaving him, for the baby we never had, for the time I wasted in the office earning money so I could buy things I did not even need. I cried out of shame for my behaviour at the office, for our clients having to witness me in this state. But most of all, I cried out of exhaustion. There was nothing else I could do – just cry and cry until I ran out of tears.'

'Did you run out of tears?' I asked Cristina with a gentle smile.

'Oh yes,' Cristina chuckled. 'After a few hours of crying, I managed to call my mother. At first, I was hesitant to call as I had ignored so many of her calls and attempts to meet over the last fifteen years. Nevertheless, I did call her and that same day, she took a train and came to visit me. At first, she just hugged and kissed me, repeatedly whispering "all will be ok, my child".'

'You seem ok to me now,' Marie said.

'I am. I am more than ok, Marie' Cristina responded with a smile. 'It will probably not come as a surprise that I was diagnosed with a work-related burnout. As I could not take proper care of myself, I was treated in a clinic. Luckily, I had the financial means to cover the expenses. At least one thing my big earnings were good for! It was a very long way to recover from my burnout. At the start, I was not able to reflect on anything at all – my mental battery was still out of the game. Only after a long treatment, I eventually regained access to my capacity to reflect and think about what to do in life.'

'And now you walk,' Marie said.

'Yes, walking helps me greatly to remind me of the beauty in life. It is in simplicity and being present in nature that I find happiness. During all those years of working, I had forgotten how beautiful the world can be, how happy life can be,' Cristina responded while her eyes sparkled. 'One day after leaving the clinic, my mother took me out for a walk. On our walk, I noticed a wooden road sign with a shell on it,' Cristina continued. 'My mother told me it was the pilgrims shell that marks the Camino de Compostella.'

'The route that you hiked in five weeks,' Marie seemed to remember.

'I had heard of the Camino de Compostella before, but never considered undertaking a hiking trip or pilgrimage of this type. Seeing that road sign gave me a special feeling throughout my entire body,' Cristina remembered. 'I can't describe to you exactly how I felt. The best way to describe it is probably the feeling of pure trust. It was a deep and pure sense of knowing.'

Cristina took a moment to think back.

'At that moment, I felt that hike the Camino de Compostella was the best thing to do for me. No, it felt the right thing to do. I took a few days to prepare for the hike and off I went,' Cristina said happily.

'Wow,' I replied. 'That is a brave thing to do, Cristina.'

'I do not consider this brave, Juliet. I have learnt that if you do the right thing for yourself, you always find a way. You will always know what to do.'

'Weren't you afraid to do this on your own?' Marie wondered.

'No, Marie,' Cristina chuckled. 'Don't forget you always have yourself with you. If you listen to yourself, nature will always be a powerful guide. You will never get lost.'

The three of us were quiet for a moment. Time passed. Somehow, the meaning of Cristina's story felt enriched by our beautiful surroundings. I looked at Marie and saw she was lost in her thoughts. I leaned over and gave her a hug.

'Shall we continue our walk?' I whispered.

Marie nodded.

'Would you like to join us, Cristina?' Marie asked.

Cristina smiled.

'Thank you for suggesting this, but I will stay up on Scarr Mountain a little while longer,' Cristina winked. 'There is nowhere else to be for me than here and now.'

'Thank you for sharing your story with us,' I smiled at Cristina, 'I will never forget it.'

'It is I who has to thank you. Thank you for listening.'

Marie and I continued our walk down the mountain. Time had passed quickly listening to Cristina's story and it seemed that both Marie and I needed time to digest her words. We walked down the mountain slowly and regularly took time to look around and enjoy the view over the Valley. We were approaching Roundwood, the destination for today.

'DEATH BY CHOCOLATE! I will have that as my dessert,' Marie enthusiastically said.

We had arrived in Roundwood and were having our dinner in the local pub.

'Did you not have chocolate cake just yesterday?'

'Mama, we have been walking for ages. I could eat a horse!'

The walking and fresh air had boosted our appetite.

'Food tastes so much better after exercise, don't you think?'

'I think so, too. And hunger is the best sauce,' I confirmed.

'What about comfort food? Where does that come from?' Marie wondered out loud.

'I suppose it depends on the individual case, but

building on the conversation we had, some people tend to eat when they feel stressed,' I explained.

'So when they have excessive levels of stress, they eat to feel better?' Marie asked.

'Do you remember Vanessa and her expensive shoes and handbags?'

'Yes, Vanessa the world traveller! When she was still working hard and feeling stressed, she felt bursts of feeling good whenever she indulged in buying something,' Marie remembered.

'Whenever she purchased something expensive, the reward system in her brain was activated and released dopamine. This gave her a burst of feeling good, which sadly lasted only very briefly,' I said. 'A similar thing happens when we eat to feel better. Eating is, as you know, important for our survival. So whenever we eat, our reward system becomes active and gives us a good feeling. It is this good feeling that also motivates us to eat.'

'So the good feeling that we have from eating is important for our survival,' Marie stated.

'True. Especially when food was scarce, the reward system motivated us to search for food so we could stay alive. Whenever we did find food, it was important to indulge as we were not sure when we would find food again. Nowadays, however, there is an abundance of food for most people in developed countries,' I said. 'Nevertheless, the reward system remains active every time we eat or when we see something nice to eat. The activation of the reward system will try to take over and convince us to eat.'

'And so the monkey will say: eat that food!' Marie chuckled.

I smiled.

. . .

'YES, it is then up to the prefrontal cortex to control your desire to eat so you won't eat too much or indulge in unhealthy eating.'

'... which becomes very hard when the mental battery has reached its limits?' Marie finished the sentence.

'When it comes to stress and eating, it can work in different ways. Due to excessive amygdala activation, the mental battery more easily gets exhausted and has no power left to control what and how much we eat. On top of that, our brain knows that eating gives us a good feeling. If we feel stressed, we might indulge in food because we have learnt that it will, even just temporarily, make us feel good,' I explained to her.

'Would you like to order anything else?' the waiter interrupted our conversation.

Marie gave me a quizzical look.

'Death by chocolate, please. Two times.' I responded.

'I WAS a little in doubt asking for the chocolate dessert,' Marie chuckled as soon as the waiter left our table.

'I know that, Marie. I believe it is important not to over-control yourself. In fact, I believe it is essential to once in a while allow yourself to eat something you really want or crave, even if it is not the most healthy option. Over-controlling your food intake can become a dangerous obsession. If you listen to your body carefully, I trust you will always find the right answer.'

'Is that what Cristina meant when she said that she had lost contact with herself?'

'I think so. When we become stressed, our monkey mind gets even more active. The hamster wheel of thoughts seems to be overtaking us. We cannot focus anymore and seem to be lost in our thoughts most of the time. We are constantly travelling in our mind and are not present in the moment. We seldom tune in to our body and notice how we really feel and what we really need. An essential part of the answer to what we really want in life and what makes us feel happy is not something that we can rationalize or put into words. It often is something we simply feel,' I tried to explain.

'I am not sure I understand. Does that mean that knowing what I want is not really knowing but *feeling*? Is this the emotional readiness?' Marie summarized her thoughts.

'Yes, you could phrase it like that. Remember I told you yesterday that our emotions are very complex. Our emotions are a collection of bodily changes, a feeling. It is by speaking about them that we try to put into words what is happening to us. But in essence, the wisdom of how we feel is in our body, not necessarily in our rationalization of those bodily changes,' I continued.

'But the brain still plays an important role, doesn't it?'

'Most certainly. Do not forget that those bodily changes are initiated by activation of certain brain structures.'

'But the feeling expresses itself in our entire body,' Marie stated.

'Oh yes. Our body contains a deep wisdom. It is an important guide in life,' I winked at her.

The waiter came back with our dessert and which we both enjoyed in silence.

DAY 3

Roundwood - Enniskerry

'No more chocolate for me!'

We were at the breakfast table of our Bed & Breakfast and I gently pushed aside the chocolate cookie that was placed on our breakfast table.

We started to eat in silence.

'Were they able to jump?' Marie suddenly asked. 'I mean, those two people could jump over the river, right?'

I was confused for a moment and then remembered the riddle about the two people standing at the side of a river. Both wanted to get to the other side of the river. There was only one boat. The boat could carry only one person. Nevertheless, both people arrived at the other side. How?

'Nope, they did not jump,' I replied. 'The river was too wide for jumping.'

'Was the river too wide for one person to push back the boat to the other person after crossing the river?'

'Can you draw this situation for me?' I asked her.

I took out a pen and piece of paper from my bag. Marie started to draw: a river, two people standing next to each other at the side of the river and a boat.

'There you go.' Marie presented me with her drawing.

'Well, let me see.' I took some time to look at her drawing before I looked her in the eyes.

'When I told you that riddle the day before yesterday,' I

said, 'your monkey mind interpreted the description that I gave to you. Based on the interpretation of your monkey, you drew a picture in your mind – a picture which looked like this.'

'The pictures in my mind looked much more real,' Marie smiled.

'The point is, your monkey mind started to make certain assumptions. Based on these assumptions, you drew this picture and tried to solve the riddle,' I explained to her.

'Are you saying that my monkey mind was not necessarily giving me the right picture?'

'Well, it certainly won't hurt to question your assumptions.'

'How do I do that?'

'Let us try this together. You look at the picture you drew while I give you the description of the situation again. Then you try to wonder whether the way you drew the situation is the one and only possible interpretation of my description.'

I slowly repeated the description while Marie concentrated on her drawing. When I finished, Marie took time to reflect.

'You never said those people were standing at the same river,' Marie suddenly remarked with hope in her eyes.

'That is true, I never said that. This is, however, not the solution to the riddle. But you do get a point for questioning your assumptions,' I winked.

'MY MONKEY still talks about those two people standing at the side of the river,' Marie said.

We had started our last hiking day. Today's hiking trail would bring us from Roundwood all the way to Enniskerry, where we would spend our last night before travelling back home.

'Let me finally tell you today how you can quiet down your monkey mind,' I replied. 'I am sure that giving the monkey some rest from the riddle will help you find the solution. Let me first tell you a little bit more about where stress reactions comes from and what we can do to reduce it.'

We had crossed another stile and entered an old forest track. The trees in this old forest are very close to one another and hardly let any light through, making the forest very dark – and especially silent. I suggested climbing the forest path in silence. I could hear the cracking of small dry tree branches and needles underneath my boots. I felt my breath and heartbeat adapting to my walking. Above all, I could hear the silence.

'So where do stress reactions come from?' Marie asked. We had left the dark forest.

'Let me explain this to you based on an example. When we do tasks, jobs or activities that we do not like, we experience negative emotions – especially when we are stuck in them for a longer period of time.'

We took a small break and drank some water.

'When we are in an environment that does not fit to us, our brain will signal this to us by producing a negative feeling, such as stress,' I said. 'The environment in this context means the tasks we do, the people we spend time with, the activities we undertake in our free time and so on. If we more closely look at who *we* are in this equation, we see our talents, our skills, our needs, our personality and our interests. Do not underestimate the importance of your interests. Even when you are good at something, it does not necessarily mean that you also like it.'

Marie frowned.

'I believe that enjoying a task is actually much more important than just being good at it. If there is a task we really like but we are not very good at, we will still experience a positive emotion which will give us energy and motivation to learn the task at hand.'

'Such as your painting,' Marie laughed.

I poked her side.

'I love painting, even though I have no talent for it. I just love it,' I said. 'In short: when there is a mismatch between what we can or want to do and the environment we are in, our brain will signal this to us with a feeling of stress,' I picked up the conversation. 'As I mentioned to you earlier, our stress eats a lot of our mental energy. After a day of engaging in a task I do not like at work, I feel mentally exhausted even before I leave work. This has nothing to do with the general demands of the task, but it has everything to do with the demands the tasks poses to me as a person with particular interests and disinterests. In this case, my mental battery is constantly dealing with my feelings of stress rather than with the task at hand. Someone else who loves that particular task might even feel energized by doing it the entire day.'

'But sometimes we have to do tasks we don't like, right? We cannot leave a job simply because there is a task we don't like,' Marie argued.

'You are right. I believe that when we know we are losing energy, I mean a situation where there is a mismatch between the environment and ourselves, we have to ask ourselves another question,' I responded.

Marie looked at me closely.

'The question we should then ask ourselves is: "Can I change the environment I am in?" If you are in a situation in which you feel constantly frustrated and unhappy, it makes sense to seriously consider choosing a new environment.'

'Such as Cristina did? She seemed very unhappy in her job and was dealing with a lot of stress,' Marie stated. 'It took, however, an extreme emotional experience for her to leave the situation.'

'We all change when we experience a strong need to change, Marie. It is only when we are open to change that we will be able to embrace it. Unfortunately, some people need to feel extremely low and unhappy to finally make a change.'

'Such as Vanessa and Cristina.'

'When we experience a lot of stress, we lose the connection to ourselves. We seem to be caught up in our mind. We are disconnected from our feelings and from other people,' I continued. 'Luckily, it does not have to be like this for everybody. If we keep our eyes, ears and mind open, the wisdom in each one of us will guide us. As Cristina beautifully said: "Why be afraid? You always have yourself with you and Nature as our guide".'

'How did you know what you wanted to do?' Marie asked curiously.

'The moment that I left my science job, I made a list of all the tasks that I did enjoy up to then. These were the tasks that I would look forward to or tasks where I lost track of time while I was doing them. This list gave me a first idea of the activities that fulfilled me. Do you have any tasks like that?'

Marie took a moment to think.

'I very much enjoy my sports. I also notice that when I don't actively engage in sports regularly, I feel as if I am sitting on hot coals,' Marie thoughtfully replied. 'I forget the time while I am reading my book or in the kitchen with you.'

'Do you like working in the kitchen?'

'Not really, but I do like to spend time with you and talk about things.'

~

'BESIDES MAKING that list of activities, I started to wonder about the jobs where those activities were useful. I must say, it was a lot about trial and error. I knew for sure that neuroscience and understanding the brain is a strong passion of mine. During the final year of my science job, I was asked to speak at a conference for coaches. They asked whether I could talk about how the brain works and how this information can be used for coaches in their daily business. In addition, they asked me to organize a workshop on the same topic. Up to that day, I had only held presentations for scientists and I had never organized a workshop in my life. Still, I took on the assignment. I remember I was very nervous. My monkey had kept me awake the entire night before the event. And you know what? I absolutely loved it. The presentation was very well received and I felt so energized after that day. That day taught me a lot about what I want to do in life.'

'So by trying out new activities, I will find out more about what I enjoy and about what I do not enjoy,' Marie said. 'What if I said that I enjoy hiking? How will this help me to find a job that I like?'

'Well, we are talking about finding your life path. There is more to this path than activities that bring you money. It is the path in life that fulfils you. To find out more how this activity can help you shape your life, you ask yourself "Why do you enjoy hiking?"'

'Because I enjoy being in nature,' Marie replied.

'Why do you enjoy nature?'

'I don't know. Being in nature makes me relax and feel good, especially when I do sports outside.'

'What else do you like about hiking?'

Marie reflected.

'We are together and we talk,' she eventually said.

'Why do you enjoy being together?' I challenged her with another why question.

'Because you are my mother and I love you.'

I smiled.

'Do you understand what I did?' I asked her.

'You asked me a lot of why questions!'

'I did. It is the why question that will eventually reveal the deeper need that drives us in our decision making and behaviour. By asking the why question, you clearly told me that being in nature and being active is important to you. We do not necessarily have to walk this exact hiking trail to make you feel fulfilled. Being in nature and being active can be achieved with many activities. It is important to find out how we can fulfil a need with activities that we can incorporate in our life. Also, you told me that love and connection with other people is an important need. By fulfilling that need, for example by taking time to walk the Wicklow Way together, you feel happy. Again, we do not necessarily have to walk this exact hiking trail to fulfil your need for love and connection, right?'

Marie reflected.

'Indeed,' she said, 'if I know that love and connection are important to me, I can fulfil them with many activities. I can make sure I spend enough time with my family and friends.'

Marie hesitated for a minute.

'By asking you the why questions, it became clear to me that you enjoy being in nature, doing sports and spending time with others, especially your family. These are a few of your essential needs that make you happy when you fulfil them, right? Even if you do not find a job where you can fulfil those exact needs, you could find a job that allows you enough free time to search for activities in nature or engage in sports and spend sufficient time with your family.'

'If that makes me happy... it would be a loss not to engage in these activities. But still I feel a bit worried about finding the right job – we spend so much time in our jobs!' Marie replied.

'Let me ask you the following question: why do you need a job?' I asked her.

'I need money.'

'What do you need money for?'

'Because I need to buy food, a house, a car,' she replied.

'Why do you need food, a house and a car?'

'Without food, I won't survive. A house I need as protection, so I guess, I also need it for my own security. If it comes to the car, I suppose I don't really need a car to survive.'

'So if I understand you right, one basic need that you fulfil by having a job and earning money is your own security and certainty, correct?'

'That is correct,' Marie stated.

'You know what? The most important thing for your brain is that this basic need for certainty is fulfilled. How you fulfil this need is entirely up to you! You are free to decide on the activities you take on as long as they fulfil the deeper needs that are important to you. What is the point of fulfilling your need for certainty with a job that you don't like? You can fill that same need with a job you *do* like and that offers you fulfilment.'

'And this will make me happy?'

'This is how one can find his or her life path. This is where fulfilment lies,' I said.

'How about Vanessa? She could not leave her job because she had bought a huge house and an expensive car she had to pay for,' Marie argued.

'Do you think your brain feels more fulfilled with a luxurious house than with a smaller, basic house?' I winked at Marie.

'But it is so nice to have a luxurious house!'

'Well, Marie, one could silently wonder whether a luxurious house is worth giving up your happiness.'

'There is no point in visiting the Himalayas if the Himalayas are not in your mind.'

WE HAD CROSSED ANOTHER DENSE, very dark forest and had arrived at The Barr where we had a magnificent view of Laugh Tay. We decided to search for a nice spot to have our lunch break. The sun had disappeared behind the clouds and a cool breeze made it a little chilly.

'What do we do when we cannot change the situation we are in? Or what if we do not want to change the situation we are in?'

I reflected.

'You mean a situation where we experience energy loss, that is to say a situation where we feel frustrated or stressed?'

Marie nodded.

'Typical examples of situations that cause energy loss in our brain are working with a colleague or boss that we do not like. Also being engaged in a job that requires skills we don't have or being in a job we don't really like are good examples. If this is the case and we notice our energy loss, we can first ask ourselves if we can and want to change the situation. We cannot change our colleagues or boss. We like to think that we can and we certainly often try, but we simply cannot change other people. If the situation becomes unbearable and seriously affects the quality of one's life, it most certainly is worth trying to find a new environment that fits better,' I explained to her. 'However, we very often have to deal with people we do not like, but not to such an extent that the quality of our life depends on those moments when we have to work or spend time with them.'

'So in that case, we do not necessarily search for a new environment,' Marie stated.

'Indeed. At that point, we have to ask ourselves a very important question. We have to ask ourselves whether we have accepted the situation just as it is.'

Marie took a moment to reflect.

'How can I accept a person that I do not like? What if that person is just not nice?' Marie wondered.

'There is a difference between accepting a person and agreeing with a person,' I explained. 'By accepting the fact that you cannot change the person, it does not necessarily mean that you agree with his or her behaviour. It simply means that you tell yourself: "I know I do not like that person and that's okay. At this very moment, I can't change him or her". In fact, if you keep on trying to change that person into a person who fits you much better, you will lose a lot of energy. The more we try to fight a situation we cannot change, the worse it usually gets. It is called the ironic rebound effect. Accepting the situation can work miracles.'

'Indeed,' Marie thoughtfully replied, 'we cannot simply change other people.'

'But we can accept them, Marie. This will set us free from many frustrations,' I smiled. 'And you know what? There is more good news. There is one person in the world that we can always influence, right?'

Marie reflected.

'Ourselves?'

We both smiled.

'Yes. We can always regulate ourselves. Self-regulation is what cultivates our freedom to decide. One fine human quality to have in our life.'

<...> *give us grace to accept with serenity*
the things that cannot be changed
Courage to change the things
which should be changed,
and the Wisdom to distinguish
the one from the other

(FROM THE SERENITY PRAYER)

A GROUP of youngsters had arrived at The Barr and decided to have their lunch break at the same spot. Marie and I put our conversation on hold. After finishing our sandwiches in silence, we checked the map together. There was one more climb ahead of us before walking down towards Enniskerry.

'Will you tell me more about self-regulation?'

We had re-started our hiking tour.

'To explain to you how self-regulation works and how we can improve it, let me go back to what I told you earlier. To summarize, I told you that our brain produces thoughts about ourselves, about others, our past and our future. The monkey mind,' I said.

'And you mentioned that it is our thoughts that lead to our emotions, our motivations and eventually our quality of life,' Marie continued.

'Also, I told you that the performance that we bring stands for the potential that we have, minus our internal blockages. The potential that we have consists of our talents, skills, expertise, experiences and interests. For many of our activities with which we can fulfil our potential, we need our prefrontal cortex. The prefrontal cortex plays a significant role in our working memory, planning and organising our behaviour, reaching our goals, learning, and so on,' I continued.

'We just the metaphor of a mental battery. When it is fully charged, we are mentally very strong and bring our best performance. But when the battery is empty, we are not really the best version of ourselves. Unfortunately, this happens mostly at times when we should experience the happiest moments of our life, such as swimming with your kids,' Marie giggled.

. . .

I LAUGHED.

'I did not enjoy that swim at all! Looking back, I can laugh about it. At that moment, I was mentally exhausted and depleted. My mental battery had reached its limits!' I exclaimed. 'Looking back at the definition of performance, many of the internal blockages that we experience are related to heightened activation of the emotional structures of our brain, such as the amygdala. If you are in a job that does not fit you at all, your brain will signal this to you with a stress reaction.'

'And when we experience strong stress reactions, we will mentally lose a lot of energy and our mental battery will be exhausted more quickly,' Marie added.

'If this is the case, we can either search for a new environment and preferably choose one that fits us best. For this search, it helps a great deal to understand yourself. To understand your most important deep-seated needs and the activities that fulfil those needs,' I said.

'And for those situations that are connected with energy loss but that we do not want to change or we cannot change, we start by accepting them – which is not the same as agreeing with them!' Marie replied.

'Exactly, this could be a colleague we work with, one of the tasks that we need to do but do not particularly like or singing in front of a crowd. There are so many situations that our monkey mind interprets as "difficult" or "stressful", which results in heightened amygdala activation,' I explained. 'Accepting the situation as it is, is already a part of self-regulation. Accepting the situation just as it is implies that we accept our own internal reaction to the situation. A situation does not exist out there but only exists in a meaningful way in our own mind. It is ok not to like a certain person or task. It is ok to feel nervous before singing on stage. It is okay to have negative thoughts about other people or certain situations. It is what it is. But what we do with those thoughts and feelings is where self-regulation kicks in. This is where we can act and take responsibility. Self-regulation significantly changes the relationship we have with ourselves.'

'Is this where it becomes important for us to be able to quiet down the monkey?' Marie curiously asked.

'It is.'

~

WE HAD STARTED a steep climb up to White Hill. Here also, we were treated to a boardwalk covered in iron wire. The wind had become stronger and chillier. I slowed down my pace and again observed how my breath and heart rate changed throughout the climb. As the fog became very dense the higher we walked, we decided not to climb further to the top of the Djouce Mountain but to walk around it right below the peak. Regardless of the fog around certain parts of the mountain, the view was simply breathtaking. We could clearly see the Irish Sea and the green fields and small villages below us. After enjoying the view for several long moments, we slowly started our descent. We were surrounded by sheep.

'When I had understood all that,' I continued our conversation, 'I started to search for a self-regulation strategy with which we can reduce our amygdala activation and at the same time give a boost to our mental battery. This is exactly what we need to unlock our potential and naturally improve our performance.'

'And to become the best version of who we are,' Marie added.

'There are many self-regulation strategies available. But there is one self-regulation strategy where those exact effects are scientifically reported. It is a regulation strategy such that when you practice it regularly, you will see two major developments,' I said. 'First of all, the amygdala calms down. This means that the amygdala will not be triggered as quickly and as intensely as it was before. Situations that used to trigger a lot of stress will not trigger that much stress any longer. Take the example of being on stage: after practicing this strategy regularly, you will not feel as nervous as you used to when you have to sing or present on stage. Put differently: the largest source of your internal blockages will become significantly reduced!'

'That means that the internal blockages become much less powerful and you more easily have access to your full potential,' Marie wondered out loud.

'Indeed. That is what unlocking your unique potential means. It even gets better. If you regularly practice this strategy, many of the cortical functions receive a significant boost. That means that by practicing this strategy, science has shown that people become more creative, make better decisions, improve their memory, improve their focus and process information much more effectively. These are just a few examples of the benefits that research has shown.'

Marie looked at me thoughtfully.

'How about your health? When we met Cristina yesterday, you said that the increase in amygdala activation had a negative impact on the immune system. If the amygdala is not triggered quite as strongly when we practice this strategy, does that mean that we do not get sick as easily?'

'We need the amygdala for our survival, emotions and emotional memory. As we discussed, when the amygdala becomes excessively activated and produces a stress reaction in our body without the presence of a real danger, it leads to a stress reaction and health problems. When there is too much amygdala activation or stress, people get ill more easily. This negative effect becomes even stronger when people start smoking or drinking alcohol to reduce their stress. Due to the fact that the excessive stress reaction saps a lot of mental energy, all the functions that draw on our mental battery basically deteriorate. Also, under stress, people are more occupied with themselves and do not really listen to others anymore because their monkey is overactive and claims their full attention.'

'And these negative consequences will evaporate?' Marie asked with a doubt on her face.

'No, that would be too much of the good news,' I smiled. 'When we regularly practice this strategy, our monkey mind will calm down - even when we are not practicing it at the moment- it leads to more serenity of the mind. Furthermore, because the amygdala calm down, many of the negative effects of excessive amygdala activation will naturally improve. If it comes to emotions, people will experience less stress, feel much less anxious and nervous. Research has shown that the general well-being, the presence of positive emotions and the quality of life improves. With respect to social skills, people will be less disturbed by negative thoughts in general and also in their communication with others. In fact, people experience more empathy in their relationships and an increase in their emotional and social intelligence.'

'What is this strategy you are talking about called?' Marie asked with curiosity.

We had descended Djouce Mountain and had arrived at a wooden bridge crossing a river.

'The self-regulation strategy that I am talking about is called mindfulness meditation,' I glanced at Marie excitedly.

'Meditation? Are you sure? This is not what I expected!', Marie looked surprised and somewhat sceptical.

I smiled.

I remembered when I had learned about mindfulness meditation during my time as a scientist. In my mind, I could still clearly see where I was sitting in my office and which article I was reading that mentioned mindfulness meditation. I had just re-read the article while my monkey was shouting judgments like: "meditation is only for esoteric people", "do not tell your colleagues about reading about meditation". My monkey was unstoppable. But I also still remember having a deeper feeling of inspiration after reading the article. It was that feeling that made me re-read that article and question my prejudices about mindfulness, a technique about which I did not know much at all,' I confessed. 'There are many types of meditation. Here, we are talking about a very specific type of meditation, namely mindfulness meditation.'

I was silent for a moment so Marie could take in that information.

'How do you practice mindfulness meditation?'

Marie eventually broke the silence.

'Aha, this is where the secret lies,' I said. 'In order to experience those positive effects, it is important that you understand the core of mindfulness practice. It is also here that mindfulness meditation distinguishes itself from other types of meditation.'

A young couple crossed the bridge and we greeted one

another.

'You mentioned that you noticed that your mind wanders a lot, right?'

Marie nodded.

'Well, in our brain we have a network that is believed to become active when we are not engaged in a particular task. As you experienced, your brain likes to wander and can trigger thoughts that are unrelated to the present moment or activity we are in we are in. This network is called the Default Mode Network. Although this network has many functions, here we focus on the part of the Default Mode Network that can make our mind wander.'

'When we practice mindfulness meditation, we activate another network in the brain. It is a network that is called the Direct Experience Network. I mostly call it DEN. The power of mindfulness lies in the fact that the Default Mode Network –the wandering mind- and the DEN cannot be fully activated simultaneously. When we activate the DEN, we will de-activate the wandering mind.'

'Will the monkey mind become quiet?' Marie wondered.

'It is also in our mindfulness meditation that we will calm the monkey mind,' I replied.

Marie remained silent a few moments and stared in the distance while reflecting.

'How do we activate the DEN?'

'The DEN is a network in our brain that is in close connection with our senses. These are seeing, hearing, tasting, feeling and smelling. By bringing our full attention to the sensory experience of one of our senses here and now, we will activate the DEN,' I explained.

'And the wandering mind will calm down,' she stated.

'And how long do you think it will take for your mind to start wandering again, Marie?'

She laughed. 'A few seconds?'

'At best,' I smiled. 'So during a mindfulness meditation practice, we consciously activate the DEN by bringing our full awareness to one of our senses. This will quiet down the Default Mode Network. Very soon, our mind will start wandering again. This is the moment that we are distracted or that our mind spontaneously presents us with thoughts or images that are unrelated to the present moment. When we notice that our mind starts to wander, we do not get worked up. We can mentally acknowledge that we notice the wandering mind and then bring our awareness back to our senses here and now.'

'I think I understand. Can you show me how to activate the DEN?'

'I suggest that we do a short exercise together. Let's sit on that big stone there next to the river.'

We found a comfortable seating position.

'There are different ways to practice mindfulness meditation, but they have a common principle: we are aware of one of our senses, this is the activation of the DEN. At a certain point, the mind starts to wander, which is the activation of the Default Mode Network. Once we notice the wandering mind, we gently bring our awareness back to our senses. No matter how long you perform this exercise, it is always these principles that guide you in your mindfulness meditation. Do you have a comfortable seat?'

Marie nodded.

'I personally find it easier to practice when I close my eyes. When my eyes are open, my monkey mind seems to be commenting on everything that I see. If this is not comfortable, you can also adopt an unfocused gaze on the ground a few meters in front of you.'

'I think I will close my eyes,' Marie said.

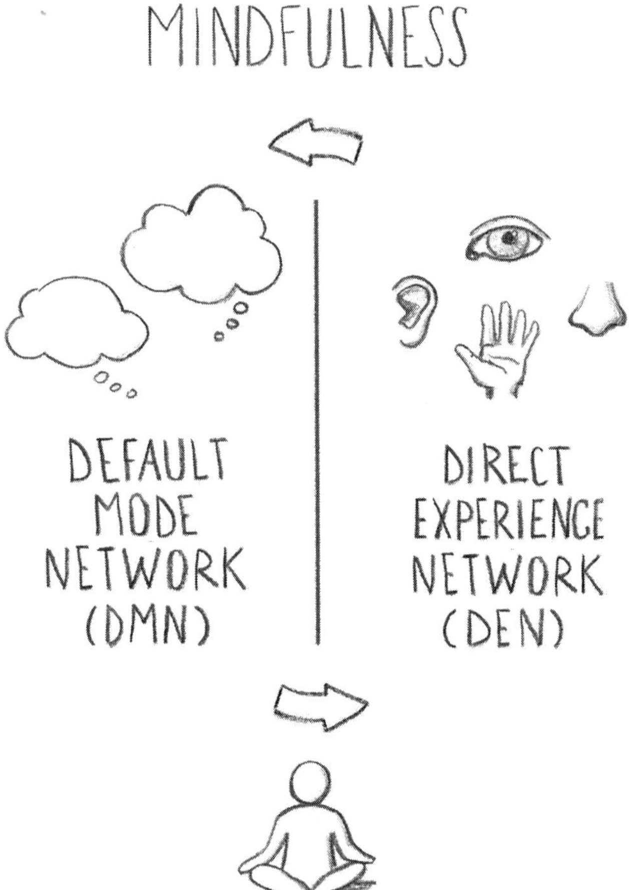
MINDFULNESS
DEFAULT MODE NETWORK (DMN)
DIRECT EXPERIENCE NETWORK (DEN)

'Make sure you are sitting up straight so you are not blocking your breathing. To get you familiar with this practice, we will active the DEN in three different ways. Firstly, we will activate the DEN through the "feeling" sense. We will do so by bringing our full awareness to the sensations that are present in our hands. We can lay our hands flat on our knees. During the first minute, we will bring our full awareness to our hands. We just feel whatever we feel in our hands without judging what we feel. Simply feeling. The moment we judge or interpret the sensation on the skin of our hands, we are engaging with our monkey mind. When this happens, simply return to the present sensations in your hands. Just feel whatever is there. Just accept whatever you feel, just as you feel it. After a minute, I will say "breathing". At that point, we will bring our full awareness to our breath. Without trying to change the way we breath, we will simply be aware of our breath. This could mean that we are aware of the movement of our body due to our breathing or simply aware of the air that is flowing in and out of our lungs. Or perhaps you are aware of the movements in your chest or tummy that are a result of your breathing. During the last part of the exercise, we will bring our awareness to sounds. When I say 'hearing', we will bring our full awareness to the sounds that reach us. We simply capture the sounds that reach our awareness. These could be sounds outside, nearby or further away, such as the river or the wind. But these could also be sounds inside our ears. Again, if the monkey mind comments on what we hear, we acknowledge its presence and bring our full awareness back to the sounds that reach us. Are you ready?'

'I am,' Marie confirmed.

. . .

TOGETHER, we performed our first joint mindfulness meditation exercises next to a wooden bridge located in the Wicklow Mountains Nature Park.

~

'THAT WAS A BIT STRANGE,' Marie smiled at me.

We had finished the meditation and had opened our eyes again.

'Strange?'

'I feel relaxed but I also thought it was very difficult to prevent my mind from wandering. It also felt as if my monkey was constantly trying to intervene,' Marie explained. 'The easiest part was the breathing part.'

'Most people who do their first mindfulness meditation clearly experience how very busy the monkey is and how easily they are distracted. We are often not aware of all the thoughts that constantly pop up in our mind and influence our feelings and behaviour,' I explained. 'Do not forget it is not about "thinking of nothing". If this intention is central in our meditation, it becomes very hard. What we do is, we bring our awareness to our sensations that are happening right here and right now. This activates the DEN. As a natural consequence, the Default Mode Network will be deactivated. Our wandering thoughts will disappear into the background. When our thoughts are taking over again and we notice, we gently bring our awareness back to the sensations we experience and of which we are aware here and now. In the end, it is an awareness exercise and not a relaxation exercise. The mental relaxation can be a natural effect of mindfulness meditation.'

'Interesting. I understand why this simple practice can be so powerful. It is our thoughts that lead to our feelings, both positive but also negative. With mindfulness meditation, thoughts are calmed down and probably trigger less stress reactions,' Marie reflected out loud.

'This is how it works. Through mindfulness meditation, the activity of the Default Mode Network will be reduced. Also, the monkey becomes much more relaxed and our thoughts will not trigger the amygdala so often and so fiercely,' I added. 'When we are experiencing stress for a longer time, the monkey becomes overexcited and it becomes more and more difficult to mentally calm down.'

'This is why it was difficult for Cristina to mentally arrive at her holiday destination,' Marie stated. 'Or see the Himalayas.'

'And this made it difficult for Vanessa to break out of her addiction to work,' I continued. 'Vanessa was totally caught up in her head. The monkey had been exposed to working heavily the last ten years, so why would it even talk about anything else? The monkey predominantly talks about work and this is what we listen to.'

'And we forget to listen to the outside world,' Marie said. 'It seems that when the monkey is very chatty, you only hear yourself and the monkey.'

'This is why people do not communicate well with each other when they are very stressed. Even more so, they listen to interrupt and not in order to understand,' I said. 'The monkey will tell you to interrupt the other person because he has something to say about the matter!'

'Yeah, I know that,' Marie smiled. 'Especially when I am upset, it is difficult to resist the monkey.'

'When we regularly practice mindfulness meditation, the monkey will calm down and we will experience a mental space in which we can choose a reaction that we find appropriate in the situation. This is not necessarily the first reaction your monkey mind comes up with!' I explained. 'When we are upset and the amygdala gets aroused, the monkey is agitated and might shout. The louder it shouts, the more difficult it is to resist.'

'When the monkey mind and the amygdala calm down with mindfulness meditation, we can decide how to react,' Marie pointed out.

'Yes, we decide. Nobody likes a boss who is out of control. Nobody likes a partner who is out of control. Nobody likes a parent who is out of control. This, Marie, is our freedom to decide. This is the space where we can take responsibility for our actions. I believe it to be one of the best and wisest qualities a human being can have.'

WE DRANK some more water and continued our walk. The Powerscourt Waterfall came into our view and I realized we were getting much closer to Enniskerry.

'How often should I practice mindfulness meditation to experience the positive effects?' Marie asked.

'Regularity is very important when it comes to mindfulness meditation. Many studies that have investigated the effects of mindfulness meditation lasted about 8 weeks. If you practice regularly, pretty much daily, it is very likely that you will feel positive effects already after a few weeks,' I explained. 'The first effects usually are the development of mental peace and calm, better sleep, feeling less stressed and agitated and behaving less impulsively.'

'So every day a few minutes like the way we did today?'

'The golden rule is: activate your DEN by bringing your awareness to what your senses are experiencing here and now, without judgement. Whether you bring your awareness to your breath or to your hands like we did, that is up to you. Many people practice mindfulness meditation by simply being aware of their breath. Other people like to practice with a body scan and others like to practice mindfulness meditation in full silence. When you try out different mindfulness meditations, you will find your own way. If you have never practiced before, I would start with 5 to 10 minutes per day. Once you feel comfortable with this amount of time, you can increase it to 15 minutes. If you eventually reach 15-20 minutes per day, that is an excellent start. In addition, I like to include a longer mindfulness meditation of 30 to 45 minutes during the weekend. Listen to your body and you will know.'

'When do you meditate?'

'I usually start and finish the day with a short meditation session. It helps me to bring my awareness to the here and now and not to get caught up in my thoughts about the past or the future. Mindfulness is about being aware of what is present here and now in a non-judgmental way,' I replied. 'It is the activation of the chatting monkey that judges everything we see or hear. By bringing our awareness to our senses and activating the DEN, we calm down the judging monkey.'

'And when we do not judge but accept what is here and now, we do not get worked up,' Marie added.

'Exactly. Also here, acceptance plays an important role. During my mindfulness practice, I accept what happens here and now. When my thoughts become active, I accept my thoughts and let them go again by bringing my awareness back to my senses. I cannot decide the thoughts that pop up in my mind or un-think them, so why fight them? This will only make it worse. Accept the thoughts that arise and gently let them go again.'

'What I still do not fully understand is how can I practice mindfulness at the moment that I am very much upset. Let us say that I have an angry discussion with someone, I cannot just close my eyes and start meditating?'

'Well you could but that might not calm down the other person,' I smiled. 'When we regularly practice, the monkey mind and stress reactions work at a reduced pace. After a few weeks of practice, you will also start feeling this calmness and serenity at times when you are not in a mindfulness meditation. This means that the monkey mind and stress levels will not be so strongly triggered in – for you - difficult situations. Of course, you will still recognize this situation as difficult, but you will feel that you are on top of it. After regular practice, you will notice that you can more easily reduce your own stress levels in difficult situations by accepting your thoughts and becoming aware of the physical changes in your body rather than getting engaged with the shouting monkey,' I continued. 'Mindfulness meditation is the practice that can help us to develop serenity in life, but there is much more to it. Through regular meditation practice, we can integrate mindfulness as a quality into our life. It will help us to live in the here and now, the only moment that exists.'

'So to find out what I want in life, I will have to explore life and try out different activities,' Marie said.

We had arrived at our hotel room in Enniskerry. I had taken off my boots and I remembered Marie's question from the first day: "Who am I and who do I want to become?". It is such a vital question that I frequently ask myself. I have come to learn it is often easier to find out what we do not want compared to what really fulfils us in life. Answering the question what fulfils me has brought me to my life path. Still, I feel it is an obligation to myself to regularly reflect on this question and re-adjust so I do not deviate too much from my life path.

'Yes, Marie,' I replied. 'Even if you do not know what you are looking for, it does not mean that you are lost in life. It means you are exploring. If you explore life, keep your senses open. Do not get caught up inside your head but approach the world with your senses and an open mind. Embrace the here and now. Embrace the wisdom of the present moment. It is only in this moment that your inner wisdom and nature can guide you. With mindfulness practice, we will more easily and clearly find out who we are and what's important to us.'

'I am never alone,' she smiled.

'You always have yourself. And nature,' I winked at her.

Marie had made us a cup of tea that I gratefully accepted. She seemed so full of energy.

'So it was because of granny's advice when you left the house that you learnt all about this?'

'Well, granny certainly played an important role here. She told me that the best thing I can achieve in life is to become the best version of myself. I have come to understand that mindfulness meditation can play an essential role in this never-ending personal development process. I like to believe, however, that I would have found this knowledge one way or another. As long as we stay receptive and cultivate an open mind, we will find the things we are supposed to find.'

'Your life path,' Marie completed.

I LAY down on the bed.

Marie sat down on the bed next to me and took out her piece of paper with the drawing of the two people standing at the side of the river. Both wanted to reach the other side. There was only one boat that could carry only one person. Still, both people reached the other side. How?

Marie fiddled around with her piece of paper. I lay down on the bed and closed my eyes. I could sense how my body started to relax.

'You never explicitly said that the two people were standing on the same side of the river,' Marie suddenly called out.

I opened my eyes and proudly smiled.

ABOUT THE AUTHOR

Karolien Notebaert is a renowned TEDxTalk speaker, bestseller author and expert on leadership & personal development. With a Ph.D. in neuroscience, she offers leadership seminars, retreats and keynotes, with 'Hack your Brain' being her most requested topic. She teaches at various top business schools world wide and received several excellence awards for her teachings.

She is the founder of the Science and Leadership Academy, which focuses on the creation of great organisations through the development great leadership.

She loves to discuss life questions, especially with her children. She is a devoted climber, hiker and runner and loves to spend time outdoors. She lives in Frankfurt am Main.

You can sign up for Karolien's newsletter here:

www.science-and-leadership.com

ACKNOWLEDGMENTS

I did not write this book alone. I feel deep gratitude for all of you who contributed to this book. This story is based on many conversations and experiences that I was privileged to share with you. You all make this world a better place!

Special thanks to my dear advisor, Christa Beiling. Thanks for your great advice, enthusiasm and trust in me. It was you who made me feel confident to start writing this story.

Sofie, I can't thank you enough. I believe you truly are a talented artist. Your designs and drawings brought this book to a much higher level and made the story complete. Thank you!

Thanks to all who contributed to the editing of this book: Bob, Karin, Paula and Linda. You all made such precious contributions to this book. Thank you Maarten for carefully reading the very first draft of this book. Not only did you provide valuable feedback, but above all, you contributed to my confidence to bring out this story.

Thanks to you, Delphine, for motivating me to join you in the library and finally start writing. I will never forget our library trips - and thank you for being my beautiful, brilliant friend.

Big thanks to my parents, my sisters, Katrien, Evi, Manon and Zoë and my brother, Filip, for your trust in me and for loving me just the way that I am.

Special thanks to my precious daughters, Josefien and Malou. Thanks for being my faithful and tireless supporters. You are a light in my life. I love the endless conversations we have and I feel grateful for all the wisdom you share with me. This book is our book.

My gratitude can not be greater for my biggest fan and support in life: my husband, Enrico. Thank you so much for your blind trust and endless support. You are a beautiful person. I am blessed to share my life with you.

HIKING

Has this story motivated you to take out your hiking boots and discover the world by foot? Well, one way is to just grab your backpack and take off. Alternatively, you can engage the cheerful and highly qualified team of Hillwalk Tours in planning your trip. Hillwalk Tours organises your hiking trips in Ireland (such as the magical Wicklow Way!), Scotland, Wales, England and along the Camino Frances pilgrim trail in Spain. I have no financial gains in promoting them, I just love working with them.

www.hillwalktours.com

REFERENCES

Notebaert, K., & Creutzfeldt, P. (2015). Wie das Gehirn eine Spitzenleistung bringt <*How the brain reaches a peak performance*>. Frankfurter Allgemeine Zeitung Buchverlag.

Baumeister, R.F., et al., (1998). Ego depletion: is the active self a limited resource? Journal of Personality and Social Psychology, 74(5), 1252-65.

Barua, B., Muchiri, M., Muenjohn, N., Burgess, K. (2019). A Model Exploring Relationships Between Positive Leadership, Meditation, Flow and Task Performance. Journal of Developing Areas 53, 229–238.

Birk, M. (2020). Why Leaders Need Meditation Now More Than Ever. Harvard Business Review.

Brefczynski-Lewis, J.A., Lutz, A., Schaefer, H.S., Levinson, D.B., Davidson, R.J. (2007). Neural correlates of attentional expertise in long-term meditation practitioners. PNAS 104, 11483–11488.

Brewer, J.A., Worhunsky, P.D., Gray, J.R., Tang, Y.-Y., Weber, J., Kober, H. (2011). Meditation experience is associated with differences in default mode network activity and connectivity. Proc. Natl. Acad. Sci. U.S.A. 108, 20254–20259.

Buckner, R. L.; Andrews-Hanna, J. R.; Schacter, D. L. (2008). The Brain's Default Network: Anatomy, Function, and Relevance to Disease. *Annals of the New York Academy of Sciences*. 1124 (1): 1–38.

Catalino, L.I., & Fredrickson, B.L. (2011). A Tuesday in the life of a flourisher: The role of positive emotional reactivity in optimal mental health. Emotion, 11, 938-950.

Chambers, R., Gullone, E., & Allen, N.B. (2009). Mindful emotion regulation: An integrative review. Clinical Psychology Review, 29, 560-572.

Chambers, R., Lo, B.C.Y., & Allen, N.B. (2008). The impact of intensive mindfulness training on attentional control, cognitive style, and affect. Cognitive Therapy and Research, 32, 303-322.

Cohen, S., & Miller, L. (2009). Interpersonal mindfulness training for well-being: A pilot study with psychology graduate students. Teachers College Record, 111, 2760-2774.

Cohn, M.A., Fredrickson, B.L., Brown, S.L., Mikels, J.A., & Conway, A.M. (2009). Happiness unpacked: Positive emotions increase life satisfaction by building resilience. Emotion, 9, 361-368.

Cooper, J. (2007). Cognitive Dissonance: 50 Years of a Classic Theory. London: Sage Publications.

Cotman, C.W., & Berchtold, N.C. (2002). Exercise: A behavioral intervention to enhance brain health and plasticity. Trends in Neuroscience, 25, 295-301.

Davidson, R.J. (2012). The emotional life of your brain. London: Hodder & Stoughton Ltd.

Davidson, R.J., Kabat-Zinn, J., Schumacher, J., Rosenkranz, M., Muller, D., Santorelli, S.F., & Sheridan, J.F. (2003). Alterations in brain and immune function produced by mindfulness meditation. Psychosomatic Medicine, 66, 149-152.

Davis, D.M., & Hayes, J.A. (2011). What are the benefits of mindfulness? A practice review of psychotherapy-related research. Psychotherapy, 48, 198-208.

Der Marshmallow Test: https://www.youtube.com/watch?v=QX_oy9614HQ

Desbordes, G., Negi, L.T., Pace, T.W.W., Wallace, B.A., Raison, C.L., & Schwartz, E.L. (2012). Effects of mindful-attention and compassion meditation training on amygdala response to emotional stimuli in an ordinary, non-meditative state. Frontiers in Human Neuroscience, 6, 1-15.

Duckworth, A.L. & Seligman, M.E. (2005). Self-discipline outdoes IQ in predicting academic performance of adolescents. Psychological Science, 16(12), 939-44.

Ehrlich, J. (2015). Creating Mindful Leaders and Organizations. People and Strategy 38, 22–25.

Emry, C.F., et al. (1994). Relationships among age, exercise, health and cognitive function in a British sample. Gerontology, 35, 378-385.

Farb, N.A.S., Segal, Z.V., Mayberg, H., Bean, J., McKeon, D., Fatima, Z. & Anderson, A.K. (2007). Attending to the present: mindful meditation reveals distinct neural modes of self-reference.

Festinger, L. (1962). Cognitive dissonance. *Scientific American*. 207 (4): 93–107.

Giraldi, T. (2019). Psychotherapy, Mindfulness and Buddhist Meditation, 1st ed. 2019. ed. Palgrave Macmillan.

Goleman, D., Davidson, R. (2017). The Science of Meditation: How to Change Your Brain, Mind and Body. Penguin UK.

Goleman, Daniel: Working with Emotional Intelligence. Bantam Books (1999).

Gottfredson, M.R. & Hirschi, T. (1990). A general theory of crime. Stanford, CA: Stanford University Press.

Gross, J.J., & Levenson, R.W. (1997). Hiding feelings: The acute effects of inhibiting negative and positive emotion. Journal of Abnormal Psychology, 106(1), 95-103.

Grossman, P., Niemann, L., Schmidt, S., & Walach, H. (2004). Mindfulness-based stress reduction and health benefits. A meta-analysis. Journal of Psychosomatic Research, 57, 35-43.

Gupta, P., Singh, S. (2019). Withholding the Wandering Mind: Examining the Influence of Mindfulness on Employees Life Satisfaction and Job Involvement. HR Journal 83–100.

Heatherton, T. F. & Weinberger, J. L. (1994). Can personality change? Washington, DC, US: American Psychological Association.

Heatherton, T.F., & Wagner, D.D. (2011). Cognitive neuroscience of self-regulation failure. Trends in Cognitive Sciences 15, 132-139.

Hesselmann, G., Kell, C.A., Eger, E., & Kleinschmidt (2008). Spontaneous local variations in ongoing neural activity bias perceptual decisions. PNAS, 105(31), 10984-10989.

Hoffman, S.G., Sawyer, A.T., Witt, A.A., & Oh, D. (2010). The effect of mindfulness-based therapy on anxiety and depression: A meta-analytic view. Journal of Consulting and Clinical Psychology, 78, 169-183.

Hölzel, B.K., Carmody, J., Vangel, M., Congleton, C., Yerramsetti, S.M., Gard, T., & Lazar, S.W. (2011). Mindfulness practice leads to increases in regional brain gray matter density. Psychiatry Research: Neuroimaging, 191 (1), 36-43.

Hölzel, B.K., Hoge, E.A., Greve, D.N., Gard, T., Creswell, J.D., Warren Brown, K., Feldman Barrett, L., Schwartz, C., Vaitl, D., & Lazar, S.W. (2013). Neural mechanisms of symptom improvements in generalized anxiety disorder following mindfulness training. NeuroImage: Clinical, 2, 448-458.

Hölzel, B.K., Ott, U., Gard, T., Hempel, H., Weygandt, M., Morgen, K., & Vaitl, D. (2008). Investigation of mindfulness meditation practitioners with voxel-based morphometry. Social Cognitive and Affective Neurosience, 3, 55-61.

Horn, Andreas; Ostwald, Dirk; Reisert, Marco; Blankenburg, Felix (2013). The structural-functional connectome and the default mode network of the human brain. *NeuroImage*. 102: 142–151.

Iwamoto, S.K., Alexander, M., Torres, M., Irwin, M.R., Christakis, N.A., Nishi, A. (2020). Mindfulness Meditation Activates Altruism. Scientific Reports 10, 6511.

Jansen, A. (1998). A learning model of binge eating: cue reactivity and cue exposure. Behaviour Research and Therapy, 36(3), 257-72.

Jha, A.P., Stanley, E.A., Kiyonaga, A. Wong, L., & Gelfand, L. (2010). Examining the protective effects of mindfulness training on working memory capacity and affective experience. Emotion, 10, 54-64.

Kabat-Zinn, J. (1994). Wherever You Go, There You Are: Mindfulness Meditation in Everyday Life. Hachette Books.

Kieras, J.E., et al., (2005). You can't always get what you want: effortful control and children's responses to undesirable gifts. Psychological Science, 16(5), 391-6.

Kober, H., et al. (2010). Regulation of craving by cognitive strategies in cigarette smokers. Drug and Alcohol Dependence, 106(1), 52-55.

Lazar, S.W., Kerr, C.E., Wasserman, R.H., Gray, J.R., Greve, D.N., Treadway, M.T., McGarvey, M., Quinn, B.T., Dusek, J.A., Benson, H., Rauch, S.L., Moore, C.I., & Fischl, B. (2005). Meditation experience is associated with increased cortical thickness. Neuroreport, 16(17), 1893-7.

Lewis, M., Haviland-Jones, J.M., & Feldman Barrett, L. (2010). The Handbook of Emotions. The Guilford Press, NY.

Maguire, E.A., Woollett, K., & Spiers, H.J. (2006). London taxi drivers and bus drivers: a structural MRI and neuropsychological analysis. Hippocampus, 16(12), 1091-1101.

Mason, M.F., Norton, M.I., Van Horn, J.D., Wegner, D.M., Grafton, S.T., & Macrae, C.N. (2007). Wandering Minds: The Default Network and Stimulus-Independent Thought. Science, 393-395.

Mineo, L. (2018). Less stress, clearer thoughts with mindfulness meditation. Harvard Gazette.

Moore, A., & Malinowski, P. (2009). Meditation, mindfulness and cognitive flexibility. Consciousness and Cognition, 18, 176-186.

Muraven, M., D.M. Tice, and Baumeister, R.F. (1998). Self-control as limited resource: regulatory depletion patterns. Journal of Personality and Social Psychology, 74(3), 774-89.

Muraven, M., G. Pogarsky, and Shmueli, D. (2006). Self-control depletion and the general theory of crime. Journal of Quantitative Criminology, 22, 263-277.

Nolte, J. (1999). The Human Brain: An Introduction to Functional Anatomy, (4th Edition). St. Louis MO:

Ortner, C.N.M., Kilner, S.J., & Zelazo, P.D. (2007). Mindfulness meditation and reduced emotional interference on a cognitive task. Motivation and Emotion, 31, 271-283.

Powell, A. (2018). When science meets mindfulness. Harvard Gazette.

Raichle, M.E., MacLeod, A.M., Snyder, A.Z., Powers, W.J., Gusnard, D.A., Shulman, G.L. (2001). A default mode of brain function. Proceedings of the National Academy of Science USA, 98, 676-682.

Reitz, M., Waller, L., Chaskalson, M., Olivier, S.,

Rupprecht, S. (2020). Developing leaders through mindfulness practice. Journal of Management Development Vol.39, 223–239.

Rook, Dennis W. (1987). The Buying Impulse. *Journal of Consumer Research*. 14 (2): 189–199

Roozendaal, B., Barsegyan, A., & Lee, S. (2008). Adrenal stress hormones, amygdala activation, and memory for emotionally arousing experiences. Progress in Brain Research, 167, 79-97.

Roozendaal, B., McEwen, B.S., & Chattarji, S. (2009). Stress, memory and the amygdala. Nature Reviews Neuroscience, 10(6), 423-433.

Schaufenbuel, K. (2015). Why Google, Target, and General Mills Are Investing in Mindfulness. Harvard Business Review.

Shapiro, S.L., Brown, K.W., & Biegel, G.M. (2007). Teaching self-care to caregivers: Effects of mindfulness-based stress reduction on the mental health of therapists in training. Training and Education in Professional Psychology, 1(2), 105-115.

Tang, Y.-Y. (2017). The Neuroscience of Mindfulness Meditation: How the Body and Mind Work Together to Change Our Behaviour. Palgrave Macmillan.

Tangney, J.P., R.F. Baumeister, & Boone, A.L. (2004). High self-control predicts good adjustment, less pathology, better grades, and interpersonal success. Journal of Personality, 72(2), 271-324.

Taylor, V.A., Grant, J., Daneault, V., Scavone, G., Breton, E., Roffe-Vidal, S., Courtemanche, J., Lavarenne, A.S., Beauregard, M. (2011). Impact of mindfulness on the neural responses to emotional pictures in experienced and beginner meditators. Neuroimage 57, 1524–1533.

Tice, D.A., et al. (2007). Restoring the self: Positive affect helps improve self-regulation following ego depletion. Journal of Experimental Social Psychology, 43, 379–384.

Wagner, D.D., & Heatherton, T.F. (2013). Self-regulatory depletion increases emotional reactivity in the amygdala. Social Cognitive and Affective Neuroscience, 8(4), 410-417.

Wagner, U., et al. (2004). Sleep inspires insight. Nature, 427, 325-355.

Watts, T.W., Duncan, G.J., Quan, H. (2018). Revisiting the Marshmallow Test: A conceptual replication investigating links between early delay of gratification and later outcomes. Psychological Science, 29(7), 1159-1177.

Wegner, D.M. (1994). Ironic processes of mental control. Psychological Review, 101, 34-52.

Wegner, D.M. (2009). How to think, say or do precisely the worst thing for any occasion. Science, 325, 48-51.

Westbrook, C., et al. (2013). Mindful attention reduces neural and self-reported cue-induced craving in smokers. Social Cognitive and Affective Neuroscience, 8(1), 73-84.

Printed in Poland
by Amazon Fulfillment
Poland Sp. z o.o., Wrocław

63211263R00081